DREAM BOLD
I DARE

Inspiration from today's thought leaders, best-selling authors, motivational speakers and world-class coaches

Compiled and edited by Carrie Stepp
Proofed by Allison Saia

Printed in the United States of America
First Printing: 2016
ISBN: 0-9967791-3-2
ISBN-13: 978-0-996-7791-3-5

Stepp Enterprises Inc. | 47724 SD Hwy 50 | Elk Point, SD 57025
Website: CarrieStepp.com | Carrie@eLearningSuccessCoach.com

This book is for

_____

With love from

_____

SPECIAL ACKNOWLEDGEMENTS

I'd like to send a special thank you to the beautiful leaders, teachers, healers and world changers, who have made this divinely guided project possible. They have trusted me with their powerful stories by opening their hearts and souls, as they share their gifts with the world in which we all share. Their stories are inspiring, enlightening and empowering, so breathe in the depth of each story, receive the messages and miracles in the making and dare to dream boldly.

TABLE OF CONTENTS

INSPIRING LIFE PURPOSE, PASSION & MISSION

ENLIGHTENING LOVE, FAMILY & RELATIONSHIPS

EMPOWERING HEALING MIND, BODY & SPIRIT

INTRODUCTION

This powerful book of transformation is comprised of 31 days of powerful life stories, intended to be savored one by one. Begin each morning or close out each day with a thought provoking message that's certain to captivate you. Get cozy, grab your favorite blanket, sip your favorite warm beverage and prepare to be awakened. There's a hero that rests deep within you. You are invited to remember. Reignite your dreams and join our unbreakable circle of love that continues to expand, as we dare to dream boldly.

YOU'RE INVITED!

You are being invited to dream boldly with us. As you step forward to take our hands and join us, if there's a moment when you feel as though declaring 100 dreams is an impossible measure, you're about to witness just a few of the dreams shared collectively within our powerful circle of love and light. As you're guided, at the end of this book is a section dedicated to help guide you, as you boldly declare your 100 dreams, to expand and awaken the power that is about to be unlocked from deep within you.

WILL YOU JOIN US IN DREAMING BOLDLY?

1. I dream to teach the world to sing, in perfect harmony.
2. I will no longer wait until I lose weight, have more time, the kids are grown, etc. No more excuses. I'm living fully today.
3. I smile, so that others may also smile.
4. I am choosing to forgive myself.
5. I pray that all of my children and future grandchildren have a personal relationship with God.
6. I am awakening my soul to its true divinity.
7. I am taking a step every day to release my fears.
8. I dream of building adult treehouses for retreats.
9. I am starting a college fund to help leaders attend college.
10. I am strengthening my relationship with my significant other by seeking the Lord, together as a couple.

11. I am debt free.
12. My children & grandchildren will always know "I want for you what you want for you."
13. I am choosing not to take things personally. I've learned it's most often not about me.
14. I am raising awareness of the dangers of tanning and funding research for alternative skin cancer treatments.
15. I am saying no to consumption and the accumulation of stuff that doesn't add value to my life.
16. I am loving the best and releasing the rest.
17. I am building foundations for schools, homes, & churches, to provide friendship, shelter, education, food/water and clothing, both at home & abroad.
18. I am forgiving the wrong that occurs in the world, while doing my best to be a catalyst for change.
19. My step-children will always know, they are loved as if they were my own.
20. I am spending at least 30 min. each morning in meditation and prayer to give thanks, before I begin each day.
21. I am unstoppable and designing a life that I love.
22. I am forgiving those who have hurt me. Instead of holding grudges, I am choosing to love.
23. I am powerful beyond measure.
24. I spend time each day to love and honor my self.
25. I am a creator of music, art and harmony in the world.
26. I am using my intuitive talents to create healing and happiness within others.
27. I am forgiving those who have made me feel small, because I am more than worthy and well able.
28. I am fully equipped and more than enough.
29. I am able to love & accept my body just as it is, at all times.

30. My children and grandchildren embrace diversity.
31. I am helping others learn they are perfect, just the way they are, as we already have everything we need deep within.
32. I have a $0 balance on my student loan debt.
33. I am getting paid to travel around the world.
34. I have a healthy balance between work, family, friends, and personal time.
35. I am serving others on a global scale.
36. I am investing in projects & foundations that serve on a global scale.
37. I am empowering young girls and women to rise higher.
38. I am forgiving myself for being my worst critic.
39. My children are grounded, happy, healthy, and following their dreams.
40. I am traveling and having hilarious adventures, both near and far, with my loved ones to make cherished memories.
41. I am turning off all electronic devices daily, to focus on spending quality time with my friends and family.
42. I am visiting all the wonders of the world.
43. I maintain a daily practice of inner soul work by connecting with God, my guardians and higher spirit.
44. I am doing what I love and abundance flows through me.
45. I am a teacher, leader, and mentor to our next generation.
46. I am nourishing my body with more water & healthy foods.
47. I am visiting my family and friends that are living in all different cities, states, countries, and continents.
48. I am developing programs for children and teens to boost their self-esteem and self-care.
49. I am teaching others how to communicate in a positive and effective way in order to receive the help they need.
50. I drink 6 to 8 glasses of water every day.

51. I own a wellness retreat that provides healing modalities such as personal coaching, Reiki, massage, facials, etc.
52. I am providing stay-at-home moms with jobs, income and more time with their families.
53. I am spending time each month with those who do not have a support system. (e.g. elderly, homeless, children)
54. I am forever young at heart, full of energy, adventure and living every moment in the now.
55. I am cooking more meals from home that are healthy.
56. I am completely and adoringly in a mutually loving relationship with my husband.
57. I am holding annual retreats abroad.
58. I am a lighthouse, a beacon of light for others.
59. I am a limitless channel of divine energy.
60. I am patient and non-judgmental regardless of how others react or what they think of me.
61. I am at a weight that is optimal for my body to enjoy abundant health and joy.
62. I have true friends that love and support me fully.
63. I am doing something to help someone else every day, no matter how big or small the act of kindness is.
64. I am seeing truth in all things and trusting what I see is real.
65. My marriage and family is my priority.
66. I am always connected to God, that guides me at all times.
67. I am running multiple businesses that provide tools for empowerment and success.
68. I help my children to value loving attitudes and positive actions above all else.
69. I am grateful every day for the gift of my body, mind, and spirit.
70. I am entitled to miracles.

71. I am helping others reconnect to the deepest part of themselves on a spiritual, emotional, mental, and physical level through music, dance, and coaching.
72. I am beautiful, glowing, radiant, and shining brightly.
73. I check in with my heart before I check in with my head when making decisions.
74. I am receiving no less than 7 hours of sleep each night.
75. I treat myself to a massage, facial, or pedicure at least once per month, with self-care daily.
76. I am investing in myself to expand my knowledge and skills.
77. I am ok laughing at myself.
78. I am taking one hour per day just for me (reading, walking in nature, journaling, taking a bath, etc.).
79. I am cleaning out my closet and life to get rid of all excess clutter that no longer serves.
80. I am visiting nature inspired locations to host creativity and writing retreats.
81. I forgive myself for making poor choices and thoughts that I was ever unworthy or undeserving.
82. I am forgiving those who hurt others, because hurting people hurt people.
83. I am going to be better today than who I was yesterday.
84. I am more than the sum of my wounds.
85. I am a source of hope for others.
86. I ignite passion and purpose with all that I am.
87. I am living every day with intention, on purpose.
88. I am serving at my highest capacity in both the professional and personal arenas.
89. I love and support my children and grandchildren in the ways that are meaningful and important to them.
90. I am open to all support and guidance that comes to me.

91. I stand fully and mighty in my divine power.
92. I have a circle of friends across the world.
93. I acknowledge the success of others every day, knowing that together we rise.
94. I forgive those who have trespassed against me and do my best not to trespass against others.
95. I am standing in my truth, knowing that as I am open, honest and vulnerable, I allow others to stand in their truth.
96. I am serving to the highest of my capacity daily.
97. I will receive all of the deepest desires of my heart.
98. I love beautiful things, which lets me know that the God within me also loves beautiful things.
99. I will love with all that I am. I will be all that I'm intended to be. I am serving with all that I have to serve.
100. I am accepting the dare to dream boldly.

DREAM BOLDLY, I DARE YOU!
This book is inspired by the 17 year old me.

WITH LOVE, CARRIE STEPP

Have you ever questioned that elusive voice that whispers so quietly from within? Where is it coming from? Is it speaking truth or deceit? Honest wisdom and guidance or false trickery? When did you first become aware of its undeniable divine presence? When you knew that boyfriend was wrong for you all along, but didn't listen? When you received that brilliant idea while taking a shower? When the unexplainable happened and your life was spared?

I'd love to hear when it happened for you, as I remember so vividly the day I recognized that undeniable, profound truth. I had traded reduced rent in exchange for painting my grandparent's home one summer. I'd spent all morning working for the nursing home, followed by a few hours working at Target while trying to figure out how I could fit in a few hours at the Dollar Store before the weekend ended, along with getting my college papers written. The truth was, several of my family members were Nurses, so everyone wanted me to obtain a degree in Nursing. They told me "it's a stable career, it pays well, it will make for a good career and that I'd be able to work anywhere." While it's a noble profession and I'm beyond grateful for all Nurses who serve, the trouble was everyone wanted it for me, except me.

For me personally, inspiration often comes in while I'm painting or creating. As I was in the backyard scraping and painting that old rugged home, I was struck by the undeniable, profound truth. I instantly knew what I needed to do, so I picked up the phone and made some phone calls. First, to my employers and then to my Mom. "Mom, I just quit all three jobs and I'm dropping out of college as I can't do this anymore." Gasping, she replied "no, you didn't" and I responded "yes I did." She stated very sternly and upset "no you can't, as you have a baby you are raising, so just what do you think you are going to do?" I replied "I'm going to apply for a job out at Gateway" (yes, the computer company with the cow spotted boxes). My mom questioned me "and what if they don't hire you?" I replied "then I will keep going back every day until they do." The next day, I filled out an application, passed the typing test and was hired before I exited the front office.

For insight, I'll keep this brief as I believe you'll be able to identify the picture. My parents did the very best they could with the knowledge and resources they had, but surviving in our childhood home was no picnic. Both of my parents had mothers that had abandoned them in their early years with horrendous stories of their own, they barely graduated high school and I was born when my Mom was 17. Struggling to make ends meet led to fighting, abuse, flying glass rages, alcoholics anonymous meetings my sisters and I were forced to attend, infidelity, and drugs to bandage the emotional scars that ultimately led to divorce. I mean no disrespect and know that our parents are proud of us, that we are loved unconditionally, and I have some good memories too; but, with little time or emotional energy remaining, my sisters and I grew up very quickly. I avoided being home and spent endless days at the library or with friends as an escape from the screaming, fighting and beatings. I craved for peace and calm amidst the crisis and chaos.

Incredibly shy and vulnerable, I fell for the first guy who paid any time or attention to me. As history would repeat itself, my daughter Ashlee was born when I was also 17. Relentlessly determined that I wouldn't allow my daughter to repeat the same childhood my sisters and I knew, it was time for me to re-write this story. Lessons are repeated until they are learned.

It was liberating to finally stand in my truth that summer afternoon with paint stained hands and ragged clothes as I set myself free from all that no longer served. With a broken wing and a prayer, the future of my daughter and I rested heavily on my shoulders. During one of my deepest, darkest nights as my daughter lay sleeping, I was feeling completely shattered, lonely and helpless. I'd contemplated giving up on life all together. Life had been pretty painful up to this point and if this was all there was, I questioned why I should even continue trying. Deep down, I knew I needed to keep doing my best, as I was all my daughter had.

In the desperation, I fiercely prayed for forgiveness and a better life for my daughter and I. The undeniable divine presence spoke very clearly to me and told me to write down my dreams. Sobbing in tears, I wrote the numbers 1-100 down the front and back sides on a sheet of paper. As I began to write my dreams, the tears got lighter and lighter until they dissipated all together. I was incredibly specific because after all, I was simply dreaming up my make believe fairy tale. While I believed most of the dreams would be impossible to accomplish, I decided I had an entire lifetime to make each one come true, which offered a glimmer of hope. The truth is, when you know what rock bottom feels like, anything better than THAT is a blessing.

Over the next few years, anytime I began to feel incomplete, I'd open my Dream Sheet, scroll through the list, locate the next dream to work on, and continue until it was achieved. Time progressed and we moved several times. A few months ago as I was decluttering and unpacking the brokenness from yesteryear, I came across that tattered, tear stained Dream Sheet again and was moved to tears as I read through the dreams one-by-one and checked the remaining achieved dreams off the list. Only two remained that were no longer dreams I needed to fulfill. Truly, our only limits are the ones we place upon ourselves!

A few items from my Dream Sheet included attending a George Strait and Garth Brooks concert, check! Obtaining a Bachelor's degree in Computer Science, celebration! Living on an acreage with a white picket fence where horses could roam, unbelievable! Traveling the world, amen! Making that outlandish six figure income, far easier than I thought! Marrying that 6'1" tall, dark and handsome husband that would love my daughter as his own? Well, when I eventually shared my Dream Sheet with him, he took out his driver's license to prove his 6'1" height to me and eventually adopted my daughter!

The truth is, my once upon a time impossible fairy tale actually came true! I hadn't realized that I'd written the script, set the stage and the plot was unfolding before my very eyes. What I once thought impossible to reach in a lifetime was fulfilled before half-time! I'm eternally grateful for the divine guidance that enters into our lives at precisely the right time, sometimes to save us from ourselves. You'll identify it when you hear it with its swift, to-the-point truth. While it may be easier to wish away the painful parts of our lives, I've learned you must pick up all of those broken pieces of glass and glue them back together as it shapes us into being the masterpieces we are destined to be.

Today, my father and I have a great relationship as neither of us are who we once were and my mother is in heaven. She was taken by melanoma skin cancer at her half-time, along with my Aunt Bev. My daughter Ashlee is healing from melanoma and I've had several suspicious areas cut out. As my beautiful Aunt Bev shared in her final moments "none of us are promised another tomorrow, so the best we can do is to live for today."

With this, I'm boldly on a mission to invest in projects that inspire, enlighten and empower this beautiful world in which we serve by dreaming boldly. The time has come for me to declare my next 100 dreams. Want to join me in making some dreams come true? I promise that all you find easy today, you once thought impossible. Find something greater than yourself that's worth investing your life in, and make it happen! I dare you to **dream boldly** and write those dreams down today.

CARRIE STEPP

As a thought leader specializing in transformative personal and professional development, Carrie Stepp is boldly on a mission to inspire, enlighten and empower the world in which we serve. She's a Midwestern country girl that's full of heart & branded in technology. As a Master Course Creator, she develops digital eCourses, presentations and products for world-class clients. She's an International Best-Selling Author, Inventor and Intuitive Creator who guides leaders in bringing their dreams to life. To connect with Carrie, visit www.CarrieStepp.com or email Carrie@eLearningSuccessCoach.com.

POWERFUL YOU

BY RHONDA CULVER

Hello, my dear friend. Come sit, I saved this chair next to me just for you. Dig your bare feet into the sand and let the grains run freely through your toes. Look out into the horizon at the blue ocean and smell the wonderful scent of the fresh water, one of the greatest life forces given to us by the Creator. Do you hear the sounds of the crashing waves and the gulls overhead? Do you feel the gentle caress of the sun peeking under our umbrella? There is nothing more serene and inspiring than enjoying and taking all this in.

I invited you here today because I am overjoyed! I am ecstatic that you have joined us in this project, this endeavor to **dream boldly.** Your success is very important to me; therefore, I want to share with you some of the challenges that you will face when you dare to live your life out loud and manifest your boldest dreams. These challenges certainly did arise for me and I want to acquaint you with them, to make you very familiar with them, so that you can obliterate and conquer them one by one.

21

Step 1: Put yourself first and acknowledge your divinity.

The first step is to put yourself first. I know at first glance this may appear selfish, but it isn't. Each of us is a divine child of the most high. As Iyanla Vanzant so eloquently puts it "You are the representation of God in your life." You must be as gentle as you possibly can to yourself. Take care of your body, take care of your mind and take care of your spirit. When your cup runneth over, you are so much more of service to others and to this world. Putting yourself first is especially important if you have been considered the strong one of your family/group, or if you're like me (in the past) you are a 'people pleaser.' In the past, I found myself doing so much for other people or organizations, that there was little to nothing left for me. Somewhere along the way, I lost me. From this day forward, I want you to put yourself first. You are to be front and center. As you filter things and requests, consider yourself and ask questions. Does this thing or action move you toward your dreams and goals? Does that little voice inside tell you, "No, I don't want to do this" but you typically say "yes" just to please others? Are you taking actions to improve your health and appearance? Are you taking actions to improve your peace and/or spirituality? Are you taking actions that will allow you to grow, to learn and move toward your passion? The time is now. Make yourself your top priority.

Step 2: Confront your fears, and then reframe them.

Fears often arise as one is on the journey to accomplish goals and dreams, especially if those dreams are bold. Fear can be paralyzing. It can stop you dead in your tracks. The strange thing is, sometimes we do not recognize fear. Life happens, and life will always happen, as we are moving toward our goals and dreams. I had so many excuses as to why I was not taking consistent action on what was supposed to be my highest priority; including deaths in the family, travel, other business priorities, family issues, etc. I chose each day to complete tasks that kept me moving forward in my comfort zone. At some point, I recognized that my excuses were just that, excuses! You are able to move toward your goals and dreams as life happens. Yes, some times may be slower than others; however, there is still movement. You must confront your fears. You could have fear of change, fear of failure, fear of what others will say, fear that you are not good enough, fear of success or countless other fears that I have not named. Take a pen and paper out and listen to that little voice inside. What are you afraid of? Listen and write it down. Once you have written those fears, acknowledge them, but don't give them power. Now reframe them and use them to make powerful statements about yourself and where you are headed. If you are afraid of failure, see yourself as successful in your goal. What are the key steps that you will take to move toward success? Recognize that stepping out of your comfort zone will be a key part of growth. Confront your fears my friend, and reframe them.

Step 3: Focus your attention on your desires.

Attitude is everything! I truly do believe that. And furthermore, I believe in the Law of Attraction. During the economic downfall a few years back, I lost all of the finances that I had accumulated. I lost nine investment properties, all of my cash, all of my retirement savings and my credit score tanked. I filed bankruptcy and my self-image plummeted. Just like that, I had hit rock bottom, or so I felt. My health deteriorated, my frame of mind was shoddy and my outlook was bleak. I spent the next several years in a business partnership; however, my focus was on 'lack' and not on abundance. I was well aware of everything that I had lost and it permeated my being. It wasn't until a chance encounter with a lightworker that a spark ignited in me, that I was not alone, and that the Divine Creator was here with me on this journey. Once I began to focus on what I wanted, and *not* on what I did not want, my whole world opened up. So for you my friend, my suggestion is pure and simple. Focus on your desires. Focus on your goals and dreams. Look at them at least weekly, if not daily. Keep your subconscious and conscious mind focused on what you desire and the Heavenly Creator and the Universe will do the rest to help make your dreams manifest. It may not be in the time that you want or plan, but rest assured, it will happen in divine time. As you are focusing on what you want, maintain an optimistic attitude. See the cup as half full, versus half empty. Acknowledge and appreciate everyday miracles, such as the sun rising and setting, the beating of your heart, or the crashing of the waves in the ocean. Have you ever wondered what incredible divine power is orchestrating all of this? If so my friend, please focus your mind on what you desire, remain optimistic and appreciative of all the blessings in your life.

Step 4: Share your goals with only those who support you.

Know this. There will be some in your life and in your circle who do not support you in dreaming boldly. Those individuals may not necessary want to bring you harm, but they may be afraid for you and/or they may be afraid of losing you. For now, if your goals and dreams are in the infancy stage, share them with only those who support you. Those who don't support you can say or do things that will cause fear, doubt or worry to arise. You don't need that right now. Protect your dreams, protect your 'baby' for now. As you get stronger, you'll be able to share your goals more broadly with confidence and the comments of others will not shake or penetrate you.

Step 5: Discipline yourself to consistently take bold and courageous actions.

This last step will provide you with visible progress toward your goals and dreams. Discipline yourself to consistently take action every week, if not every day, to move you toward your goals and dreams. Each week, define 3-4 tasks you plan to complete and complete them. Make at least one of those tasks outside of your normal comfort zone. Remember, you are the one who defines which dream(s) are your major priority for now. The dreams can be related to business, family, spiritual, etc. Whatever it is, make a choice and move towards it. Discipline yourself, take consistent action and make it happen!

I am here for you, my friend. Call me if you need me. Thank you for sitting with me and soaking up the beauty of one my most favorite venues on the planet, the beach, and enjoying the natural beauty that the Divine Creator has gifted us. Make it a wonderful day, week, month and year. **Dream boldly** and accomplish those dreams, because **you** are powerful!

I would like to acknowledge Christine Salter, Orgena Rose and Salpie Tatka, angels who have crossed my path and shared key insights with me. I would also like to thank Tonna Korsmo for introducing me to Christine Salter. Last but not least, I'd like to thank the Coach Extraordinaire Vanessa Shaw for insights that she shared at her yearly Big Bold Event.

RHONDA CULVER

Rhonda Culver is a personal finance professional, author and speaker. Upon exiting a 20 year corporate career as a finance executive in corporate America, she established a career in real estate investments. Prior to the housing crash, her net worth was near $2M when she was forced to file bankruptcy. Turning her financial condition around equipped her with lessons learned, and the knowledge and desire to instruct others on successfully improving their finances. She credits her turnaround to listening to the whispers of her soul and daring to **dream boldly**. Learn more at www.RhondaCulver.com.

I AM HOME

BY ELISA JOY TORRES

Have you ever had the feeling of being slightly off-track, yet continue clicking along at a rate that told you, you were getting somewhere fast, but it might not be where you truly wanted to go? Have you ever woken up in the middle of a dream to find that the place you were dreaming of, was the place you belonged? When you awoke, it felt like it was supposed to be a fuzzy dream within the dream, but it was your reality. Have you ever felt like that?

I lived this way for more than four decades. From my earliest childhood and into adulthood, my marriage, children, homeschooling, hobby farming, and the busyness of living a life that required moving (at last count) 29 times. I woke up every day knowing that Home was not where I was. Yet I was never fully cognizant of how to define where Home was. How does one define something that one has yet to experience?

My wake-up moment shook me to my core a few months ago, when I finally realized the extent to which I had allowed life and relationships to happen *to* me, rather than *for* me. Up to that wake-up moment, if a person wanted to have a relationship with me, I would look at all the ways I might adjust myself and my preferences to fit that person into my life. Then I would overcome any misgivings in the name of "Christian love" and go ahead and welcome them into my world. I never once considered that I had the right, let alone the responsibility, to place boundaries upon others. I simply responded to what crossed over my own blurry boundaries and into my space with what I had been taught was "love." I never considered that in order to love others effectively, I must first love myself to the extent of knowing when to say "No" unequivocally to that which makes me uncomfortable, triggers my defenses, causes my GUT (God Uttering Truth) to turn cold, or steals one iota of magic from me.

In this way, I allowed life to happen *to* me. And I felt it was simply my lot to respond to it in ways that I considered beautiful. Anything else was frowned upon as unfeminine at best, and unChristian at worst.

I married the first man who told me I was the one for him. I refused to consider that he might *not* be the one for *me*. And he wasn't. But I adjusted. For 24 years, I adjusted. I adjusted so much and so often that I never allowed myself to become fully myself. I poured myself into making sure he, and then our children, found joy, peace and fulfillment in their lives and I told myself, "I am happy doing this. This is my calling. I am fulfilled."

All the while, time was speeding by, years were drifting into oblivion, and I was waking up in the misty tendrils of dreaming dreams I could not embrace, longing to be somewhere I'd never known. Home.

I began to sense that there was more to life for a woman than clicking along "doing" religion, marriage, and raising kids into adulthood. Everyone knew that I was here to serve and could be counted on to "Git 'er done" for one and all; for all except me. It wasn't that I didn't count. Rather, my personal definition of "counting" in life was based upon how effectively I could be there for others, so that they might feel more fulfilled in their own lives. I was dedicated to making everyone around me more comfortable.

I continued to the point that I spent my life apologizing for my idiosyncrasies. Was I too loud? "Oh, I'm sorry!" Too funny? "I'll calm down, sorry." Too smart? "I'll pretend to be fascinated with what you are saying, even though I just did the research that proves you are dead wrong." Too bright? "Oh, sweetie, I'm sorry you have to squint when you are around me. Here's a pair of sunglasses. I'll try to tone it down." Now I have a hashtag I use that makes me smile so wide, that I laugh every time: #bringyourownd***sunglasses. Yes, bring your own damned sunglasses, because if I *am* too bright for you, you may want to keep moving on. I've learned that my adjusting to others' comfort zones serves no favor to them, nor myself. It simply delays the realization that we may not be of one another's truest tribe.

Here is the Christianized version of what I learned about the Golden Rule and it has changed my life forever. This revelation has released my I AM to the place where I have begun to realize that it is within my power to solidify those dreamy tendrils into a new reality for myself. What is the Golden Rule? "Treat others as you would wish to be treated" is one version. Another is "Do unto others what you would have them do unto you." or "Love your neighbor as yourself" may be the version you grew up with, if you have religion in your roots, as I do.

Here's where we go wrong with this idea, if we choose to only see it from one perspective. In order to treat others with the love, respect, and honor that we wish for ourselves, we must first learn to love, respect, and honor ourSELF. "Love your neighbor as you love yourself." There's a stipulation there, and most of us miss it. **You** come first. Knowing yourself. Honoring your I Am. Loving your *self* so that you may then know fully how to love others. Intimacy with yourself is your key to loving others. It is also your key to finding Home.

It was mine. I was in a very emotional conversation with my former significant other while he was packing to leave me for the fifth time in three years. My honesty and my raw, unfiltered "brightness" had blinded him once again and, instead of discussing differences, he was packing up and leaving my life for a few weeks, allowing things to "blow over," to then return when he felt "safe" again. I told him "Why leave? Stay and let's talk this out like adults. You'll be back. You always come back." To which he replied, "Then don't let me come back."

No denial. No insistences that he would not return. Just, "Then don't let me come back." I realized in that moment how much I had become a person who "let" life happen *to* her instead of making choices for myself and then walking out of those choices, come what may. I realized in that moment that it was time to change. It was time to unpack my dreams to say "Yes!" to them, allow the Universe to unfold details for me, and start manifesting the life that I truly wanted. It was as if the proverbial lightning strike happened right then and there, and I suddenly felt so overwhelmingly homesick that in the next few days it became a physical pain in my body. I wanted to come Home. To my self.

I was living in Kansas City, KS where I had moved to live nearer to my partner. He had become not only my romantic partner, but also my business partner. I knew full well how this would pan out. He most definitely would be back and he would have a short list of how I might do better in getting along with him. Except this time I would not be there. I would be doing no more adjusting for anyone else in order for me to fit into their life.

I was moving on. And I sensed a deep need to be free from all of the accoutrements of my former life that I had been moving with me wherever I went. The furniture, décor, even the appliances all had to go. I didn't know why or how or where I was going, I just knew it was time to lighten my load.

Within a few short days and after much prayer, meditation, and confirming talks with my most trusted mentors, I packed up all of my most important possessions, sold all of the furniture, and prayed with all my might for guidance on where our next destination would be. All I knew for sure is that I had to be in a place saturated with love and laughter, music and prayer. A meditative place. A place in the woods under a massive amount of sky, a home flooded with light of every kind. That's all I knew for sure.

Three days before we were to be out of the rental home, with all of my earthly possessions sold and gone, and surrounded by packed and sorted boxes, I received a call from a missionary friend who asked me if I would like to rent their sweet home in my hometown two hours away. A furnished home. A home whose walls are literally soaked in decades of love and laughter, music and prayer. A little four bedroom cottage in the middle of hundreds of acres of woods and streams, with a benevolent sky smiling down upon it all. Three days before our departure date. Door number one: opened wide!

Door number two: I needed a job. I landed one seven minutes away within seven days of my arrival. The numbers three and seven have long been special to me and here they were. Faithful and true as ever.

Door number three: Here I am pursuing several dreams at once as God continues to pour ideas and blessings into my path. I'm also putting my self first and allowing others to come and stay, or to squint and depart as needed. I hold my friendships loosely, stay unapologetically true to my own nature, and I accept others right where they are, just as I allow myself to be exactly as I Am; raw, funny, loving, even angry or sad, but always honest.

I feel as if I have finally found Home. I feel as if my train has clicked back onto a track that has me clipping along at a fascinating rate. My dreams are no longer tendrils of a vague memory as I awaken; rather, they are becoming more and more solid and tangible every day. I have found my Home. But it is not this cottage. It is *me*. And I am deeply grateful.

ELISA JOY TORRES

Having attempted life as a caged bird, one day Elisa ventured outside her cage and discovered life was far more enjoyable without those bars of conformity, and she flew. Twenty-three years as a career wife, foster parent and home educator have equipped her uniquely as a parenting mentor, intuitive, and relationship coach. Elisa is a gifted actress, voiceover narrator, singer/songwriter, advertisement writer, and life coach. She encourages being unapologetically, uniquely you as she dug deeper and discovered her great I AM, and has finally found God within. Connect with Elisa: ElisaJoyTorres@gmail.com.

REFLECTIONS

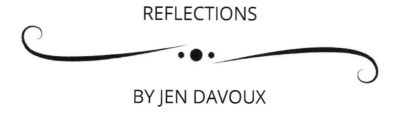

BY JEN DAVOUX

As I sit here reflecting on my past few weeks, my heart is still captivated by the beauty of Hawaii. My husband and I visited the beautiful island and I'd like to share a glimpse of what I discovered, felt and seen. How truly treasured and chosen are we, that the same God that created the mountains and oceans, the green valleys and the galaxy full of brilliant stars; that He looked at you and me, and knew we needed to be part of this masterpiece too!

As I climbed the mountain, fear began to creep in. I mean, we were extremely high up, and any wrong turn could have sent us tumbling down. I needed to breathe out that fear and keep my eye on the prize, as I knew the view from the top would be glorious. And it was! From below, who would have known what was waiting on the tip-top of that mountain, as a galaxy of stars and lights reflected such beauty.

As I swam in the ocean and embraced the waves, I gripped my feet in an attempt to jump the wave, but a majority of the time, the waves would wash over me as I inhaled the salty sea. In fact, a few times those waves swallowed me up underwater and like a fish, drifted me up to the shoreline full of sand. Looking back at my husband and friends standing there in the ocean jumping waves peacefully, was very humbling. I had thoughts of wishing I was a little taller, and the thought of being a little heavier crossed my mind for a second. I questioned how I might stand firm during those waves. Alas, I didn't let height nor weight stop me, and I knew I had to get up and walk back into the ocean, sand and all. The waves needed to be conquered, I needed to learn the timing of the waves, and I needed to plant my feet firmer. As I walked back in, my friend offered me her hand. That's all I needed.

As I walked up the trail to the lighthouse, I stopped several times, not only to enjoy the view, but also to secretly take a break. I was pondering how much longer this steep, straight up climb could possibly be. You see, although the view was wonderful, it took my full determination and willpower as every corner was another mile up! What kept me going was that inner curiosity, that inner hope, that promise of knowing the lighthouse was awaiting me!

Finally, there it stood perched in the midst of rocks, blue water all around. A house that shines in the middle of the night, the everlasting lighthouse! The breathtaking views! You can't help but wonder of the story behind this spectacular lighthouse. Who were the hands that built it? Who dreamt this miracle into form? Years after it was handmade, crafted into its permanent position, it still shines with the dream and purpose behind it!

As I flew over the island in a helicopter, I saw mountains, waterfalls, fire burning on the ground, destruction from the volcano, black ash layered over the Earth, and green lush vegetation climbing up deep valleys. I was reminded of God's perfect plan. You see, everything flows together. The nature of life presented before us intertwines with who we are; our emotions, spirituality, and our minds, living out day to day.

We have all stood on a mountain high sometime in our lives. Things were good, exciting and all coming together perfectly. It is so much easier to praise God in those moments. To see the positives and breathe in all that is given. We have also had our shares of the ocean waves crashing all around us. There are days it's difficult to stop and catch our breath before another crashing wave hits. We have all been in droughts, where the agony and pain isolates us from everyone and everything. When you felt as though there was no hope, because you couldn't feel beyond that moment. You were so thirsty, yet didn't have the energy or time to pick up the cup and drink from it.

At times, there can even be those deep valleys where it feels as though there's no way out. The sun may not rise high enough to shine brightly in the valley lows, but if you look to the right or to the left, there is a mountain that overlooks the valley.

Amazingly enough, from way up there, the view is beautiful and the sun is shining bright, awaiting for the perfect time to peek some sun rays into the valley.

As I peered out the window and witnessed the majestic rolling hills, the pilot said, "Let me show you something that very few will ever get to see," as he turned that helicopter around and flew straight down into the valley. I embraced the moment as a whole new meaning stirred within my soul.

Life may place you in the middle of a deep, dark personal valley. You feel lost, discouraged and it paralyzes the mind. It can bring forth defeat, feelings of shame and make you want to stay in hiding, as you simply want to close your eyes and give up. But, the next time you are in the valley my friend, please embrace it. Grow in it. Observe all that you were unable to notice before.

As the helicopter descended, to our surprise, in the middle of this valley was a hidden waterfall. A miracle! Looking from the outside in, you'd miss it, but being up close in the deepest part of the valley was something unexpected that flowed so freely. The pilot swooped in, up and all around the valley. He said, "Watch this," as he flew the helicopter up the green valley wall, until we saw the tip of it, followed by endless waterfalls.

You see, standing in the valley will only last until you notice the unexpected blessing. Take one step at a time as you let go of all that hinders you from rising and trusting that there's more. There's always a way out, up, over or through it.

God is everlasting! He is by your side, going before you to prepare the way, and behind you pushing you along the way. He wants you to focus on him, what He can do for you, and what He has done in your life already. "God's love for you never stops nor fails" (1 Corinthians 13:8). It's everlasting! So pause and take a look at who you are, the progress you've made, and reveal the grand purpose of your life. Regardless of any situation you are in, how many times you've messed up or given up, He will always refresh your soul and fill it up, if you allow Him to.

My husband, Devon, kept saying during the helicopter ride, "All of this can be painted into canvases." All I could think was that yes that's true, but the canvases have already been painted! We are looking at them, and we are living them out. Today, yesterday, it's only a small dot on the big canvas that God has painted just for you, and for me! Surrender, run and just be enough! It can be the opening through which the whole panoramic view of your life is seen. "Greater is he who is in me, than he who is in the world" (1 John 4:4). Yes, in any given circumstance you can surrender, you can run, or you can climb upon God's lap because He knows you are enough.

Let this be your resting place, your place to be filled with restoration, hope, peace and of Him. Be confident in knowing you are never alone. God is your strength! He can heal any broken heart. He will forgive. He will embrace. And, He will love you no matter what! No matter the size of the wave. No matter how hot that lava feels. No matter how low the valley is. No matter how high the mountain is. Go ahead, grasp how wide, how high, how long and how deep the love of Christ is for you. You are blessed my friends.

JEN DAVOUX

Jen Davoux is an inspirational writer, co-author and speaker. She's the wife of a Pastor, has four children and is a successful business woman, operating an organization with Young Living. She equips families for life-long transformation with nature's gift of wellness using essential oils, tips on abundant health, and obtaining financial freedom. Her mission is helping people "see" and unveils their full potential. Following God is far more valuable than all the riches of the world. She walks beside you to unshackle scars and lies to bring forth the light and hope of your true purpose. Contact Jen: http://yl.pe/48p8 ID: 1500731 or aseedwithin1@hotmail.com.

BELIEF IN YOURSELF MEETS BOLD MOVES

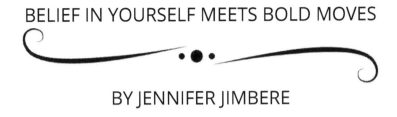

BY JENNIFER JIMBERE

Several times in our lives we come to a fork in the road. What crossroads are you facing right now? Are you debating a major career move? Perhaps your relationship is on your mind and you're trying to decide if you should stay or leave. Maybe it's time to decide how to make yourself more of a priority.

Change can be a daunting task for many of us, but I can tell you that when you take that leap into what is next for you, it is absolutely worth it. The good news is that contrary to popular opinion, change doesn't have to be as hard as you may think.

So often we are told that being an entrepreneur is a constant struggle, but I'm here to dispel that myth. There are times when I am so happy being my own boss that I wonder what I'm doing wrong since I had this perception that it should be a daily battle between me and my business. At least that's the warning I got when I took the bold leap to leave my cushy corporate job. Then I finally realized, there is no value in manufacturing a struggle just because I was told that's how it works. As I coach women, I realize many aren't comfortable in simply enjoying the ups and downs of entrepreneurship and unknowingly strive for being frustrated.

What I do know is that it takes bold decisions and belief in yourself that you will succeed. It takes confidence in your abilities, persistence, hard work, and most of all a consistent positive mindset.

My own fork in the road came just over a year ago, when I needed to decide if I was going to stay in the corporate world or invite myself into my own business. I was not 100% fulfilled even though I enjoyed my responsibilities and the people I supported. I deeply desired to have an even greater impact on more people to help them unleash their strengths.

Dreaming boldly came not from a place of deficit, as I was already actively coaching in the corporate realm and compensated for my impact. Instead, it came from a place of possibility. I had a front-row seat to the incredible power of coaching, as I witnessed my internal team unlock possibilities for themselves. Seeing this over and over unlocked something inside of me and all of a sudden I started imagining the possibilities presented before my family and I. I began dreaming of all the professionals I could positively impact for expanded possibility.

It would have been comfortable for me to stay at my current level, to continue receiving annual promotions, or to move into different roles, but instead I chose to make a bold move and took the leap!

I wanted to guide more than one organization at a time and to help so many more clients. I knew something had to change, so I gave up what I "should do" by staying in my safe, corporate job, and went after what I really desired.

Since I already had a sense of confidence given my corporate coaching role, I was aware of the business results and worth I was able to deliver. I made a bold declaration and decided to apply those processes to my own business. I would leave certainty behind for the unknown. I truly believe that when belief and bold moves meet, magic happens!

I believed that owning my own business would allow me to work from anywhere. I saw it as a fulfilling proposition, because I could support strong leaders in need of a confidant outside of their organization to help them flourish into their ideal leader self. Plus I would ignite a spirit and knowing that people are creative, capable, wise and good! When you're chasing that outcome, how can struggle even be seen?

When I left my corporate role, I talked with my spouse about launching my business. As a previous bank manager who had been in the financial services industry for almost 20 years, I knew what it would take for this to work. Leaving a very healthy salary behind and jumping into the unknown, we made a bold decision to make it happen.

We lived in a beautiful community, a very desirable area, where builders would frequently leave flyers or knock on our door. You see, this was our 5th home and it was a 55 year old brick bungalow, but that was not their attraction. It was the size of the lot we lived on and the many possibilities for building an expansive house with a high profit turn around. While there had been several knocks on our door, hearing the pound on our old wooden door really didn't interest us, until our decision was made.

Most people aren't willing to make bold moves, such as selling their dream home, to start a business. They get stuck sitting on the fence of uncertainty. Being comfortable is an easy choice, but I was prepared to write the next chapter of my story and willing to step outside of that comfort zone. We believed I could do it. There was no plan B. Everything I had learned up to that point had prepared me for this bold move.

My belief is that we are all creative, capable, wise and good. That's the message I had boldly preached in my corporate roles, so I had to believe it to be true also for myself. That belief continued to filter into my thought process and my mindset around my capabilities and true potential.

I'd like to share a helpful tool that I picked up along the way. The 90 second scorecard was shared by an incredible speaker at a conference I coordinated, and it has stayed with me ever since. When challenges arise, many people stay in that problem for far too long, unable to see what is available to them. What the speaker shared that I immediately implemented, and wish to share with as many people as possible, is the 90 second scorecard. When a problem presents itself, picture a scorecard or take a piece of paper and draw a line down the middle of the page. On the left side is the perceived problem. Begin writing out all of the reasons the issue is bad, who it affected, what you could have done differently, etc. Instead of continuing to write out all of your concerns indefinitely, set a timer for 90 seconds. After 90 seconds, switch your pen and focus to the right side, where the possibilities exist and begin writing out the opportunities available for you to move forward. You will soon begin to shift away from the problems and train your brain to look for solutions.

This tool even guided us in making the decision to sell our dream home. It was a booming housing market and most homes were selling over asking price or experiencing bidding wars. After doing the math, realizing how much the business would be to professionally launch, we made a plan and executed. Together, we decided to sell our home, capitalize on the market and move. We packed up our family and moved to another city where the housing prices were not as high, purchased a newer home on a golf course and provided the structure for the business to thrive during its infancy.

Know that if you have a solid vision of what you want to create, and the belief that you are capable of bringing it to life, it can be a positive experience. One of the reasons people often do not go after what they really want is a lack of confidence. While confidence isn't an area I struggle with, I do know that you have strengths within you to unleash and take on bigger challenges than you may presently believe.

My encouragement to you is to take the steps needed to make a bold decision, whatever that looks like for you and trust in your abilities. I invite you to invest in you. The confidence will come as you take action and find your path. Begin creating a plan and go all in. No more waiting. We need you to shine your light, to believe in yourself and to stay positive. There are a lot of people waiting for exactly what you have to offer!

One way to stay positive and to boldly keep moving forward, is to make an inventory of all of your strengths and review it daily. I invite you to sign up to receive my free video series on Positive Psychology Principles at my website. The principles will increase your positive emotions while supporting your **bold dreams.** What bold move is waiting for you to own? What you believe is possible is only the beginning!

JENNIFER JIMBERE

Jennifer Jimbere is the President of Jimbere Coaching and Consulting and Co-Founder of The Radical Joy Seeking Women's Club. My vision is to inspire individuals, teams and organizations to unleash strengths and maximize performance with proven, action-oriented, research based applications in coaching, change management and positive psychology practices. With over 13 certifications and degrees, and 17 years in learning and development, Jennifer helps people move forward with lasting change, to build their competitive edge, and to live their best life now. Learn more online at JimbereCoachingAndConsulting.com or RadicalJoySeekingWomen.com.

ALWAYS BELIEVE

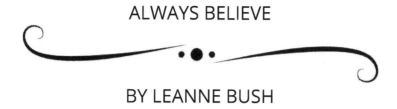

BY LEANNE BUSH

Believe. I didn't always believe and my life reflected that. A few years ago, this simple word appeared to me and since then I've seen it everywhere. I still see it all the time. I have surrendered and now have "**Believe**" all over my house in various forms. It is now my new motto. Since accepting this word into my life, I've conducted some research on the law of attraction and gratitude. They are both connected with believing.

I still have struggles in my life, but I also have victories too. I give all things to God, believe, and when He answers my prayers, I thank Him for everything. I've decided to further pursue my writing in various forms, personally and professionally, and God is helping me do that. I believe He is directing my steps and I try my best to follow the path I am shown.

My advice is to never give up and to always believe. Follow your dreams, believe, and you can accomplish anything!

LEANNE BUSH

Leanne Bush is the Author of four published books, a blogger and songwriter. When she's not writing, she's a crafter and seamstress, crocheting and sewing heartfelt quilts. She's married and lives in Iowa. Her published works are available at LeannesHandiwork.com.

THE JOURNEY TO RADICAL JOY

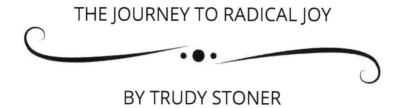

BY TRUDY STONER

I've been working with women for over 10 years as both an esthetician and a coach. Upon spending a lot of time talking about life, it wasn't long before I noticed a very common theme. It really didn't matter if I was talking to someone younger, college aged, women close to my age, or those much older than me. I repeatedly heard "I feel like something is missing." "There must be something more." "I just want to be happy." "I want to make a difference."

Same desire, different women, day after day, week after week, all the time. It was heartfelt and so very common. I identified with these women, because we were all singing the same song. Everything I was hearing was exactly what I'd been yearning for myself. To be sure, the time I spent in the treatment room of the day spa, working with women is what opened within me, the desire to become a coach. It was this message, this desire, which led me to dive deep into Spiritual Psychology and Soul Centered Living. I wanted my work to have meaning, and to make a difference. Little did I know that my quest for knowledge would lead me back to my very beginning, would lead me home. Everything I was searching for was literally inside me all along. I wish I could have pointed these women inward then, to help them see that everything they desired, they already possessed.

It is our innate nature to be joyful, but life can be hard, and messy and we are not always taught to seek joy as we are growing up. More often than not, as adults, we must re-teach ourselves, or better yet, erase the messages that have been programmed into us since childhood. Don't get me wrong, I'm not saying that we've all had "bad" childhoods or parents, that's not it at all.

Very well meaning parents and role models unknowingly taught us to be wary of our innate well-being and joy. Not consciously of course, but because that's how their parents taught them, and society as a whole has continued to support and teach certain beliefs. These beliefs are not very conducive to joy.

Here are some examples;

If you are a confident child you are taught to be humble, not to toot your own horn or brag about yourself.

If you are pretty, or attractive, you better not let anyone know, or you risk being perceived as conceited or stuck up.

If you laughed to loud or got really excited, you were more than likely told to quiet down, to be respectful.

In her book, Goddesses Never Age, Dr. Christiane Northrup explains it like this; "We've been taught that anything pleasurable is suspect. We say "It's a guilty pleasure," "It's sinfully delicious," or "We're having too much fun." Someone is "drop-dead gorgeous," or we're going to "die laughing." These sayings are based in the idea that we can't handle the fullness of someone's beauty or our own laughter. The thought of simply enjoying ourselves and savoring sensual experiences, makes us look over our shoulders for the pleasure police."

Very well meaning adults simply taught us not to have too much fun, to be fearful and to watch our step. How many babies and toddlers do you know that struggle with joy? In trying new things, feeling confident, sharing their accomplishments and grinning with pride? At what point do we stop cheering them on and begin teaching them to downplay their accomplishments lest they be seen as boastful? It's time we reclaim our joy.

We need to go within, to heal without. Think back to when you were a child. Were you encouraged to be yourself, to let your light shine? Was there laughter in your home, play, fun and lots of love? That's exactly what's been locked up inside. Laughter, play, fun, love, energy and light. If you really want to find your joy, go back and rediscover these innate qualities. The ones you were born with, that used to come naturally, that you were "taught" out of.

So, how in the world do we do that? Well, it's simple actually. Almost too simple. To heal without, you must go within. Simply quiet the mind, relax, and allow yourself to remember who and what you are. That's it. And yet, as simple as that may sound, often it isn't very easy. We need guidance, direction and support, which is exactly why I created The Radical Joy Seeking Women's Club. It is beautifully designed to be a journey to joy, to self. A resource for women longing to create a life of balance, joy and well-being. I've made it my mission, passion and purpose to create what I longed to find.

I imagined a source of encouragement, resources and online learning. I was excited to reach out to other coaches, authors and experts to interview and feature within the club. Little did I know that the dream I had back then, was just a small seed, a tiny speck compared to what was about to transform.

I reached out to an acquaintance with the intention of inviting her to be one of my guest experts. We had a few calls to get to know each other, shared ideas and discovered what we were each doing within our businesses. I was impressed with her knowledge and her willingness to simply brainstorm ideas with me. When I spoke with her about the club, it was to ask her to occasionally write an article or two. Well, let me tell you, she shared my vision and passion and before I knew it we were off and running, ideas flying so quickly we could hardly keep up!

Deciding to take The Radical Joy Seeking Women's Club to a completely new level together, was a dream come true. I'd been working and coaching on my own for so long, I'd forgotten how wonderful it felt to work with someone who shared the same dream, the same vision and just when I thought it couldn't get any better, it did!

The psychology and coaching pieces were covered between the two of us including; relationships, change management, business, and a host of other topics, but we didn't have an expert in the field of health and wellness. We didn't want just anyone. We wanted a coach that really understood the importance of wellness from the inside out. We desired a holistic approach that included mind, body and spirit. We went on a quest, and began searching for that perfect someone until we found her. When we approached her, she said that we were an answer to her prayer. Little did she know, that is exactly what she was for us.

Together, we joined forces, began to create, dream, discover and expand. What we dreamed together is now a beautiful online community for women, created by women. We have proven that each day you dare to connect with your inner greatness, take action and follow your heart, there are no limits to what you can create and share with the world.

Do you have a dream you are holding within? Do you also feel as though there must be something more? Are you longing to discover and connect with who you really are? Are you waiting for permission to shine? Today, do something wonderful. Do something that makes your heart sing. Be still and patient, and your true self will reveal herself to you, I promise. Give yourself permission to shine, to thrive and take the steps you need to step into your greatness as you make your dreams come true.

Syd Banks shared it well when he stated "You see, where we're searching for is our home grounds. We're searching to find the way home, and to find the way home, what you have to do is look at everything in reverse. Because naturally, if you're away from home, if you keep walking, you walk further away. To find home, you've got to turn around, and instead of searching outside for the answer you seek, all you need to do is look inside. There lies the secrets that you want." Quote shared from Michael Neill's book "The Space Within." To begin your journey to awakening joy, I invite you to look within, connect, learn and grow. Begin living a more mindful, meaningful life today!

TRUDY STONER

Trudy Stoner is a Transformational Coach for Soul Centered Living with certifications in holistic and stress management coaching, business and life. She's the founder of Mindful Resources, an online education center for anyone seeking to live a more joyous, mindful life. She's a resident expert and co-founder of The Radical Joy Seeking Women's Club, an online subscription community whose mission is to empower women worldwide to take their personal growth to heart. Her passion is the study and teaching of Spiritual Psychology. She's a writer and presently working on her book, A H.E.A.L.ing Process. Access free resources at www.RadicalJoySeekingWomen.com.

DREAMING THE IMPOSSIBLE

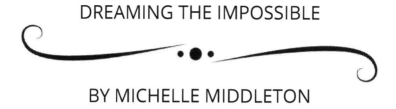

BY MICHELLE MIDDLETON

I was homeless when I began building my online business. It wasn't pretty. In fact, it was horrible. The crazy thing is, I thought I was doing all the right things in order to build a successful coaching business.

Shortly after my wedding, I was laid off from my six-figure sales position. At the time, I wasn't concerned as I'd never had a problem finding work. Over the course of nine months, I applied for hundreds of jobs, including those paying $11/hour and yet, I never received a call back.

This equated to no income coming in for myself and my husband, so our finances dwindled faster than we could keep up. After nine months of this scarcity driven lifestyle, we ended up living in a tent.

I don't need to go into the details to share with you how humbling our crisis was. We owned a 16-man tent that we tore down, moved, and reassembled each and every night for months on end, which felt like forever. We were clearly not living the lifestyle of the rich and famous!

During the nine months that I watched our savings dry up

faster than the Sahara Desert, I was doing absolutely everything I knew to bring in money through my coaching business.

As instructed, I was posting on social media all day, every day. I signed up, and followed every freebie I could find, thinking this is how a business was built, and that I could figure the rest out all on my own. I was engulfed in information overload and overwhelmed.

Finally, a very generous coach reached out to me, and offered me a spot in her program. This was the turning point in my life and business. The lessons I've learned from absorbing every drop of knowledge from my mentor have been priceless.

My life is nowhere near perfect today, but at least I'm not where I used to be. The trajectory of my business is quickly climbing for the greater good of all, and I now have a larger following than I ever dreamed possible. I no longer live in fear of where my next meal is coming from, and each day I vow to take one step out of my comfort zone. Life begins at the end of your comfort zone. I believe in living with intention and on purpose as you celebrate the climb.

MICHELLE MIDDLETON

Born and raised in Seattle, WA, Michelle has evolved as an expert in the field of Outside Sales. After more than 20 years as an Award-Winning Salesperson, Michelle began a sales and success coaching practice to empower women to sell with confidence. Michelle lives in Austin, Texas with her two daughters, and three dogs. Learn more by connecting with Michelle Middleton, Success and Empowerment Coach on Facebook, or at MichelleMiddletonCoaching@gmail.com.

FREEDOM LIKE A BUTTERFLY

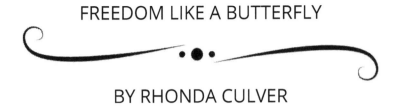

BY RHONDA CULVER

As I journey through life, it is clear to me.

I must be like the butterfly, God intended me to be.

Free to journey over oceans afar.

Free to roam with no fear of a scar.

From the lashings and critical judgment of others.

For God made me special, unlike no other.

So why do I fly now with clipped wings?

Why am I fearful to open my mouth and sing?

Why not float and flutter and experience the world freely?

Why not let my voice ring and explode gleefully?

I see ahead my wings extending proudly.

Me opening my mouth and sharing my voice loudly.

I will walk the path, but each step is not yet clear.

I do know, it starts in this moment right here.

I have made up my mind and I will do it.

I will devise a plan and carry myself through it.

One day my friend, you will find and you will see.

I spread my wings and I am free.

Like the butterfly, God intended me to be.

RHONDA CULVER

Rhonda Culver is a personal finance professional, author and speaker. Upon exiting a 30-year corporate career as a finance executive at accounting industry firms and American Express, she established a career in real estate investments. Prior to the housing crash, her net worth was near $2M when she was forced to file bankruptcy. Turning her financial condition around equipped her with lessons learned, and the knowledge and desire to instruct others on successfully improving their finances. She credits her turnaround to listening to the whispers of her soul and daring to **dream boldly**.

Learn more at www.RhondaCulver.com.

BE BOLD, BE STRONG, BE YOU.

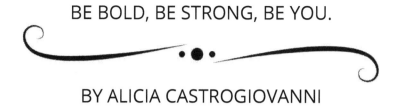

BY ALICIA CASTROGIOVANNI

"Oh my God what just happened?" I asked myself as my shaky hand reached for the gearshift. I quickly parked the car. I could hear the rapid beating of my heart through my chest. The windshield wipers still swishing back and forth, I took my trembling foot off the brake pedal and quickly turned on my emergency flashers. I fumbled through my purse, trying to locate my cell phone to call home. My car had spun out of control, hitting a guardrail, and was now parked underneath an overpass on a one-way lane facing oncoming traffic.

"I am going to get hit. I am going to get hit. I am going to get hit," I repeatedly thought to myself. "What if no one can see me around this bend? What just happened? I am going to be so late for work! How am I going to afford to fix my car? Could I die sitting here? No, I'm fine. I'm OK. I'm not hurt. It's just the front end of my car. Why did this have to happen to me? Is this really my life right now?" So many thoughts raced through my mind in a matter of seconds.

It was around 7:30am on a weekday at peak rush hour. The

first few vehicles quickly slowed down. I could see their brake lights reflecting off the puddles on the road. One car pulled over to a complete stop with just barely enough room for another car to pass between us. A man quickly jumped out of his vehicle and approached mine as I rolled down my window. "Are you ok?" He asked. "I think so. I am not sure what happened. I was driving and out of nowhere my car just spun."

"It appears that you blew your back tire. I am an off duty officer. Let me stop traffic for you so you can pull out and we can get you to a safer area. Are you ok to drive out of here? It's tight but you have enough space to pull forward, cut your wheel and reverse back around."

"Yes, I think I'm OK. Thank you so much." He walked in front placing himself between my car and oncoming traffic. As he held both hands up over his head, I drove my car out from underneath the overpass and was able to find a gravel parking lot nearby. The officer followed me to ensure my safety. He asked if I would be OK and did I need further assistance. I thanked him for his time and service and let him know I had my cell phone and could call AAA for roadside assistance. I reassured him that I was able to get in touch with my mom and she would be picking me up. As he left, I took a couple deep breaths and called home.

That was the beginning of a series of events that would eventually lead me to question my purpose, spirituality, and my desire to live a meaningful life. I remember thinking to myself, "Is this really all that life is?" I had just graduated with a Master's degree five months prior to the accident. Graduating with a Master's degree after only two semesters should have been an honorable accomplishment. Instead I left school feeling empty, lost, confused, lonely, and helpless, with no clear direction. I questioned my field and my major. I had just spent thousands of dollars and five years of study on a degree in a field I felt no motivation to pursue a career in. I felt guilty for even wanting to consider something else. I had gained twenty pounds, just to lose thirty, because of depression. I questioned friendships and relationships that I had cherished and valued throughout college. I started to push everyone away. I felt very misunderstood and forgotten by God. In addition, I was physically ill and doctors would tell me nothing was wrong; their solution was prescribing antidepressants.

My rock bottom wasn't an isolated moment, but a series of ups and downs over a period of several months. After the accident, I quit my job two weeks later, called my then boyfriend to tell him I was moving back to North Carolina, where I attended grad school. I packed everything I could fit into my baby blue Chevy Malibu and left my home state of New Jersey, the town I called home for twenty-three years, to start fresh somewhere new.

Two months after moving, I clearly remember the first day I walked into a local contemporary church. I felt hopeless and desperately wanted answers to why I felt so lost in my path. Alone and unsure of what to expect, I listened to the sermon and let God love on me through the pastor's words. I broke down in tears and surrendered. I cried for almost twenty minutes straight. I was grateful that the lights were off so no one could see my swollen eyes and blotchy face. I knew in that moment that I had to let go of control and expectation of what I wanted my life to look like. I told God that I needed Him and wanted to serve to be used to do great things.

Since that day, I continued to experience one trial after another: heart break, making new friends, looking for work, quitting jobs, starting new ones, getting fired, living on my own, finding roommates, learning to take care of my health and exercise, managing my budget with very little income, and the list goes on and on. Each trial I experienced in my twenties taught me something new about myself. My ability to let go and seek God has allowed me to grow in ways I never could have imagined as I sat in my car that rainy October morning.

If you are going through a time where you feel like you just can't catch a break, let me encourage you. As long as you are here, your story has not ended. There is still time to press forward. My mission is to help others uncover their identity that can easily get lost in the hustle and bustle of our daily life. Remember that you are unique and no one else is created just like you. You are precious and you have a gift to share with the world. Let your light shine. Your hardships will only make you stronger. Be Bold. Be strong. Be You. "I believe every soul has a desire to move in some way, it's just a matter of finding the way that best works for you." Love, Alicia.

ALICIA CASTROGIOVANNI

Alicia Therese is a passionate dancer and dance fitness professional, focused on deepening the connection between mind, body, and spirit. She does this by creating a space for self-reflection and conversation with her participants, walking them through easy-to-follow movements aided by meditation and music. As a dance fitness instructor for the past 7 years, Alicia believes that everyone can find freedom in one's own form of movement. Her artistic inspiration originates from her own relationship with God and her love for many world cultures and rhythms; including Latin dance, Indian Bollywood and African step. Learn more at AliciaTherese.com.

LESSONS IN LISTENING

BY ALLISON LINDGREN

Sarina's big, beautiful blue eyes smiled up at me as I stood in the church she loved, beside the table that honored my oldest sister's life. The photographer had captured the spirit in her eyes so perfectly it made my heart ache. Feeling the sting of tears, I looked away, turning to the urn that held the remains of her earthly body. The shades of opalescent blues and greens swirled like waves around its gleaming, ginger-jar shaped curves. Our mother's silver filigree cross necklace draped around its neck and bore testimony to the faith that that was so important to Sarina.

I knew my parents planned to leave a single red rose on the table beside the urn, but the long-stemmed peach rose with a small butterfly attached was a surprise. It was that little butterfly that touched me most. Knowing that her struggle with the darkness of depression was now over, I reached out to touch that little butterfly and whispered softly, "Fly free, little butterfly. Fly free."

Sarina and I grew up together, only sixteen months apart. We came as a pair to many people, especially when we were little. To most people, we were 'Sarina and Allison.' To those closest to us, we were "Trina and Ally." To our dad, we were "Punkin' and Dumplin'." For a while, it seemed you couldn't have one without the other. We were best friends who fought like crazy. But we knew that in new situations, we'd never be alone. And we knew if we had each other, we'd always have a friend.

Even through her own struggles, Sarina was an avid and non-judgmental listener, and the person with whom I could share my innermost hopes and dreams. Yet, when fierce storms raged in my life, I withdrew. This was no new strategy for me as I'd done it all my life. When I told Sarina I couldn't talk because I couldn't stand the pain, she respected that and backed off. She knew I'd talk when I was ready, but she never stopped calling or sending encouraging e-mails and notes, letting me know she was there when I could talk. Except she died before that happened, leaving me with much regret. I had two thoughts immediately after I heard she was gone. The first was, "How will I ever get through this without her?" And the second was, "How could I ever have wasted so much time?"

I struggled as I weathered the storms in my life, but Sarina's death seemed to be too much. My faith and relationship with God had always been so important but as I struggled, I became angry with God and I pushed him away. So used to drawing from His strength, my new anger only intensified my hopelessness.

That year, in addition to the other battles we were waging, our family lost nine members, including my sister and my husband's mother.

As I lost my footing emotionally, I lost my bearings at home, at work and I got mired down in the daily act of living. "Dreams are for other people, not me anymore," I told myself. "I'm older now and it's time for me to be practical." Thankfully, God wouldn't allow me to wallow in my world of self-pity. He started moving in my life, in wonderfully imaginative ways, to show me that His plan for me was much greater than I'd ever have dreamed on my own.

His messages started with butterflies, with the first significant butterfly coming at Sarina's funeral. Butterflies started appearing everywhere. God used what I would listen to, where I was, to get through to me.

I remember one horrendously hopeless day. Seated in a swivel rocker, I watched with detached interest as butterflies flitted from flower to flower in the garden below me. Dropping my head in my hands, I sobbed, and then heard a tap on the window. I stopped crying but didn't raise my head and then heard another. Tap. Tap. Tap. Raising my head, a large Monarch butterfly was fluttering at the window in front of me. I watched for a while and then opened the book I'd sat down to read. I looked up every now and then to see that the Monarch had settled itself on the windowsill. That butterfly stayed with me all afternoon as I sat and read my book.

Then, not long after my uncle's funeral, I was seated outside in a circle of loving cousins. As a group, we'd recently suffered many losses. We were grieving for dads, uncles, cousins and sisters. As we sat in that circle, we watched as a Monarch butterfly entered, and slowly made its way past each person in the wide circle, before finally joining another butterfly just beyond us. As I shared my butterfly stories, a cousin who was also mourning his sister, smiled as he shared what I hadn't seen. These two butterflies had flown a straight, determined path together, down a very long, country driveway before joining our group. They knew where they were going!

Conveying the real emotion in these messages is difficult, but as hard as it was to go through this, it's also the time I started to hope again. To dream again. I made reservations for a work conference and attended a life-changing seminar by Stephanie Staples. In an interactive presentation, she joined the audience, asking about our biggest dreams and where we wanted to be in five years. Then, she asked the hard question, giving us time to think without giving excuses. "So, what's keeping you from achieving that dream?"

Just before leaving for the conference, I'd ordered two books to read on the trip. One was called, "The Butterfly Effect:

How Your Life Matters" by Andy Andrews. Andrews shares that the decisions we make now and the way we treat others has more impact than we'll ever know. I read his words, "You've been created in order that you might make a difference. You have within you the power to change the world. Your life and what you do with it matters forever." As butterflies kept appearing in my life's most important moments and in my reading, I realized that God was speaking to me and I learned to pay attention to those inner promptings and that still, small voice.

"You're Made for a God-Sized Dream" by Holley Gerth helped me recognize that pursuing God-given dreams is not selfish. They're the dreams He placed in my heart and He gave me a purpose to fulfill. As another little push from the Spirit, my sister-in-law added a line to her e-mails that read, "Each of us is created and placed here by God at this particular time in history, in this particular place, and given a role by God that is given to no one else."

Two weeks after that conference, I gave up a corporate job and set out on a new path, pursuing something completely new and foreign. It was exciting, but I was scared to death. That's when God started to bring Sarina to me when I was sleeping, to deal with the fear I felt as I started to dream more boldly. Sarina and I sat together in the dream, side by side, as she reviewed the plans for my book while I shared problems I hadn't solved yet. I came away from that "business meeting" with several solutions found.

God taught me lessons when self-doubt was hindering my progress and I wondered why He'd use *me* for this project. There had to be people more worthy and gifted than I was. Sarina came back to my dreams again with messages so motivating and so personal to me, I'm unable to share them. It's like sitting down with your sister for coffee, except the conversations are deeper in both thought process and meaning. Through the years, I've learned to accept fear and walk through it anyway; because we all know that if your dreams don't scare you, they aren't big enough.

My most valuable lesson while learning to **dream boldly** and fulfill His purpose is learning that He'll use whatever He needs to, to get my attention, tell me He loves me and bring me back to Him. During the storms, He used time, objects that held a special significance to me (butterflies), people, music, books, dreams and a lot of necessary inner-work, to bring me back, to work out His purpose. I just had to learn to listen.

ALLISON LINDGREN

Allison Lindgren is a newspaper feature writer, columnist and transformational author with over 20 years of business management experience. With an educational background in management, she's fiercely committed to guiding business owners and leaders to achieve workplaces that are highly engaged, energized and committed to company goals and values. Her mission is to help businesses transform their workplaces by raising their employees up, enhancing employee retention and morale, and increasing production and profits. Learn more at AllisonLindgren.com or RaiseThemUp.net.

BREATHE IN BOTH WORLDS

BY ELISA JOY TORRES

I am a being of diverse parts.

Once fractured; healing, choosing now.

Parts that are to remain, and parts that must depart forever.

Birthed into deep, paradigmatic waters.

Forced to swim in violent currents;

currents both mine, and not mine.

Foreign tides swell and lift me to the air I breathe,

then undertow engulfs, buries, and consumes.

Until I wonder; am I truly a creature of this swelling,

massive place?

Or a land dweller, lost at sea?

Clarity is hard to come by when one is continually swamped

in chaos of reckless dichotomy.

I have often glimpsed the hope of salvation.

Having climbed onto the floating things that others ride,

for a ruse of safety.

I imagined fully escaping what feels like a watery grave.

In those times, the very salvation I reach toward,

becomes the fragile raft that mercifully

breaks apart beneath my weight.

Dumping me into safer waters,

where alone and floundering,

I finally learn to swim strong

in the ecstasy of revelation.

That I am a creature,

who is still breathing,

and becoming glorious

in both worlds.

ELISA JOY TORRES

Having attempted life as a caged bird, one day Elisa ventured outside her cage and discovered life was far more enjoyable without those bars of conformity, and she flew. Twenty-three years as a career wife, foster parent and home educator have equipped her uniquely as a parenting mentor, intuitive, and relationship coach. Elisa is a gifted actress, voiceover narrator, singer/songwriter, advertisement writer, and life coach. She encourages being unapologetically, uniquely you as she dug deeper and discovered her great I AM, and has finally found God. Connect with Elisa at ElisaJoyTorres@gmail.com.

GUIDED BY LOVE

BY KARA STOLTENBERG

What if you had a blank page? What if you could use any medium you wanted to create upon your page? And let's just say you had easy access to receive support from the most talented artists, creative designers and skilled writers to bring this magnificent creation to life. What if you knew exactly what you wanted to put on that page, but were too afraid to do so?

Suppose you let others put their thoughts and ideas onto the page, even the ones you didn't like. What if you didn't feel worthy to ask for assistance, even though it was freely offered? Imagine if you let that blank page sit, neatly tucked away in your closet, for fear that you might ruin it or waste your only chance to make it great?

At every crossroad, life is a blank page. What are you going to put on yours? What dreams do you have locked away in your heart waiting to be tended, unleashed, and liberated? What are you waiting for? You are here on this planet in a body with unique abilities and passions, desires and design for good reason.

Those things you long for... you know the dreams I'm talking about... the ones you buried deeply when you thought life said, "No!" The heart longings you let go of when your world came crashing in around you... the ones you stopped letting yourself dream, because it hurt too much. It was actually heart-breaking to hold them any longer, so you let them go. You convinced yourself you'd be fine without them, and you embraced other endeavors to try to forget about your heart's desires. But the *deepest* longings of your heart never really go away. You know this. They aren't meant to be forgotten. They never will go away. They will either die within us, holding us captive and likely in pain, or they will find freedom in living the life you are here to live.

. . . . .

After what felt like a miserably failed attempt at the one dream I wanted more than anything in life, I made a conscious decision to kill the deepest desire in my heart. In some ways, I was being practical. It seemed realistic to me that I was not succeeding at this path so I should switch gears and try another one. So I did. I stopped dreaming about an expanded family. I stopped dreaming about a husband with whom to share my life. I reasoned that this was simply not happening for me, so I buried my deepest longing. It seemed to me that my only choice (*you never have only one choice*) was to grow in gratitude and foster contentment for the beautiful family I did have. I deliberately let go of the hope for more. It hurt to want more. It was painful to hold on to the dream. I wholeheartedly wanted to enjoy the life I had, so this seemed like a sensible road for me to travel down. And it appeared to me the only way I could open myself to dreaming other dreams. This is somewhat comical to me now that I understand I can have lots and lots of dreams all at once! Denying the fact that you want something doesn't actually lessen the fact that you want it.

On the surface, my plan worked for a while. Certainly it worked to cultivate an even deeper gratitude as a mother and brought more joy and contentment into my life. My coaching business expanded and I was tapping into my soul purpose more than ever before. I was giving it attention, thinking creatively and allowing it to fill my heart in a different capacity than I had done in the past. I designed new programs, listened more attentively to the needs of my clients and got creative about how I might be part of meeting them. In the back of my mind, I thought perhaps when my son graduated (which would be more than ten years later) I would consider giving the path of love another chance. Presently, the very thought of that plan makes me laugh out loud! But at the time, I thought I finally had it all figured out. It felt safe, and I needed it to be safe.

Then one day, I realized I wasn't being honest with myself. I opened my heart just enough to acknowledge that the protective barrier was only keeping me from enjoying life to the fullest. *My life!* It dawned on me that I could dream a hundred other dreams and create endless beautiful things, but this desire for an expanded family was still very much alive in me. And as it was, it was painful. It felt like a loss. I came face to face with a very courageous decision. I could either continue to bury the dream because I was afraid of more potential hurt and heartache or I could dream it. I could open to my heart's desire.

Ironically, when you want something so much, it hurts to hold onto hope for it. For some strange reason, it feels like wanting it moves it farther away. This could not be further from the truth! You think that if you close off your heart, you can avoid the pain, but by doing this, you actually put yourself in a perpetual state of pain. The truth is, wanting something is the first step to creating it. Actively owning and cultivating your desire for something, is the beginning of allowing it into your life.

At first, re-opening to this desire seemed like it was going to be easy. I felt ready to be part of a very different kind of love that was in alignment to my heart. However, I didn't know that I needed to deliberately dream about what I wanted. I simply opened my heart to the idea of love. What followed was a series of dating adventures that invited me into deep healing work. Though the experiences seemed difficult at the time, the healing that occurred for me was both beautiful and necessary. Moving through the depths of that healing journey set me up to dream. Indeed, I had a blank page in front of me and I could design and create the vision for what I wanted. I could teach myself to align with and be informed by the truth of love, or I could surrender to fear and be misinformed by old experiences, past pain and the beliefs I had adopted into my subconscious programming because of these hurts. The choice seemed an obvious one, but the continuous effort to align with and be informed by love, is beyond courageous.

Probably requiring bravery at my highest ability was the shock that as I opened my heart to dreaming, grief emerged. Not just a few tears, but a deep well of sadness. As I admitted to myself and verbalized to others how much I wanted these things, I needed to cry (again) over not having them. Re-opening my heart to the desire cracked open the pain of not having what I wanted more than anything in life. I had to go back into the depths of that pain. It hurt. It felt risky. Sometimes I wasn't sure it was worth it. I think this may be why we try to keep our deepest desires at bay. Somehow we know that to dream creates longing, and longing pokes at the well of tears that have been dammed up instead of cried out. Crying the tears was an important part of letting go. In my tears, I was letting go of the pain of the past and opening my heart to be guided by the truth of love. You have to cry the tears, to feel the depth of joy and open to something new. You have to believe that you are worthy to have the deepest desires of your heart, even after the hurt you have experienced. Opening your heart is the only path to love and though it feels vulnerable, it is worth it.

In this dance between grief and gratitude, it was like the dreaming taunted me, accusing my contentment of being false. I had done so much work to be truly content and happy with my life as it was and I was afraid to feel a hole in that happiness as I began an honest declaration of these dreams. I kept asking questions. Can I be alive in gratitude and contentment while also owning my desire and dreams for more? I asked for Divine guidance to hold this dream and instead of associating sadness over the lack of not having it, I wanted the supernatural ability to delight in the mere thought of my dreams coming true. I honored the grief as it came up and simultaneously asked for the ability to feel true joy for what is and what is to come.

It was a continuous realignment to love. As you open your

heart to desire, the pains of your past hurts emerge, giving you the opportunity to feel them, reflect and let them go (again). This is the heart of healing. The truth of love is something that your soul knows. If you keep aligning to it, love will enter your life in a hundred ways every day. Fair warning however, that the space between hope and grief is not for the faint of heart. This is where your bravest self has to be willing to step up. You have to believe that love will indeed triumph, because it will. Every time. And if you are open to love, it is yours.

For me, with the passage of time and conscious effort, grief subsided, gratitude and contentment for my presently beautiful life grew and I began actively and boldly declaring my dreams for more goodness! For the first time in my life, I am completely confident that these dreams and desires will bloom into reality! I have learned to align with the rhythm of love no matter the swirling of outer circumstances. Things going on around me simply give me the opportunity to bring the inner truth of love to the world. At our very soul essence, love is the only truth. Aligning with love creates the safest and happiest adventure in life. Not to mention that the experience of being alive is so much better when you are dreaming! I smile more often, as if I hold a precious secret. I am more attuned to the sacred connection I have with beautiful souls that cross my path, to the ever present assistance of a loving God and the entire universe at my back. This is living the truth.

To dream is a sacred form of soul art. From this moment forward, your life is a blank page waiting for creation. I invite you to ignite your imagination with the deepest desires of your heart. Honor your soul's longings to be alive! Let go of your inhibitions and fears, the mental blocks that make you want to hold back. Put to rest the voices that say you will only be disappointed if you open to your deepest desires. For your deepest desires are where the magic lies! Your best life is waiting for you. Go ahead and dream!

KARA STOLTENBERG

Kara Stoltenberg, MA, Ed., is an international best-selling author, master teacher and intuitive mentor dedicated to helping people realize healing through self-love and self-respect. Through online communities, live events and individual work, Kara creates a safe, supportive environment for people to make tangible life changes. She empowers you to dream your dreams and implement simple practices to align with them coming true. If you are ready to remember your true value and make changes within a supportive community, visit KaraStoltenberg.com.

STEPPING INTO MY LIGHT

BY KIRSTIE DEMPSEY

When I was a little girl, I remember endless days of staring out my bedroom window into an open field, day dreaming about what was possible for me. I dreamt of being a doctor helping out sick children, as patients looked at me in admiration with eyes full of love for the live-saving work I completed. Or of being a secret agent and saving the day, by rescuing a fellow agent in distress.

Looking back, it's quite amazing how big my dreams were. In my dreams, I was decisive, powerful and always the hero. But in real life, I was lonely. I felt like I never quite fit in anywhere. I was always the girl that was picked on at the sleepovers. No, really, one of my most horrible, vivid memories from junior high was from a sleepover. I had become the victim of the horrible three-way-calling fad. You know, the one where someone calls you and there's secretly someone else being quiet as a mouse just waiting to pounce at the slightest wrong?

I was always quite the diplomat, never choosing one side over the other. This made it a bit more challenging for the girls in my grade to pin me as the gossip, but it sure didn't stop them from trying. I remember one night, the one that triggered a chain of events culminating to the infamous sleepover incident, sitting at the computer desk in my family's living room. I was having a chat on MSN Messenger with some girls in my grade when the phone rang. It was one of the girls I was chatting with, calling to share the latest gossip about a mutual "friend." I couldn't tell you now what the context of the call was, but I do know that her chatter was met with a lot of "oh really's" and "oh wow's" on my end.

You see, since childhood I have been extremely un-opinionated. To a fault, in fact. In my early 20's I couldn't even have told you what I preferred for dinner because I was so used to putting that decision onto someone else. It wasn't that I didn't care what I ate, it was because growing up, I was trained to believe that what I wanted came last to what everyone else wanted. After enough times of voicing your opinion and it being ignored as a child, you kind of just give up on having an opinion. For the longest time, I thought that was a strength.

I was flexible. I was adaptable. I could be anything to anyone! But, it wasn't long after I had my son that I realized that the qualities I had told myself were strengths, were making me feel weak as a mother, as a woman and as a human, that longed for more.

Giving birth to my beautiful son somehow switched

something on inside of me. I had to be the rock. I had to be the strong, decisive woman I was always meant to be. My husband was working a job at the time that required him to be away for 24-36 hours at a time. There was nobody to turn to when it was decision time. It was time to become the decision maker.

On September 3, 2015, my son's first birthday, something shifted within me. I should've been overjoyed, celebrating with friends and family at the party. Instead, I was putting on a smile while wondering deep down what the hell I was doing with my life. I can still see myself putting on the dress I had bought just for my son's party. Busying myself all morning in the kitchen, baking beautifully decorated cakes and making sure I had just enough balloons ready to decorate the room. I was doing what I did best, keeping myself busy, and subduing the ever-present voice in my head saying, "there is more for you."

A month later, I was boarding a plane with my son for a two-week stay with my grandparents in Florida. I was armed with *The Desire Map* by Danielle LaPorte, and a newly lit fire under my ass to find my life's purpose. Now, for any of you who have embarked on the journey of finding your life's purpose, I'm sure you know how long and winding this journey can be. I thought I would complete the workbook, decide what I wanted to "do with my life" and things would be rosy. Can I get a heart-felt LOL here?

What actually ensued was another year plus of soul searching with immense up ups and a few downs along the way. But what I can say standing here now, nearly a year and a half later, is that this is by far the greatest journey I could've ever chosen to take. I've come to realize that this life we are given is truly a beautiful journey. It is meant to show us how to love fully, be the light and have a ton of fun along the way.

My story has now come full circle. I understand what happened the fateful night of the three-way call. An easy target was spotted and taken advantage of. I didn't love myself. In fact, I didn't love myself until very recently. I didn't feel I was worthy. I was never enough. And, everyone around me could sense that. The result of that three-way call was an invitation to a sleepover where I was humiliated by a group of a half-dozen girls for agreeing that another "friend" was a "slut." I spent an hour crying my eyes out in the bathroom, and was eventually saved by a fellow earth angel, who came into the bathroom with a telephone, even though everyone told her not to. She told me I was beautiful, even while bawling my eyes out, and rubbed my back while I called my parents to come pick me up.

Beautiful sisters like her, who have recognized me for who I am and encouraged me to step into my light, have changed my life forever. This year alone, I have been blessed with friendships that have expanded me beyond anything I could have imagined was possible for me.

My true turning-point came a mere two months ago when I was introduced to a woman who has gifts beyond this Earth. She taught me how to love myself unconditionally, and that no matter where I came from, I always have a choice to be who I want to be in every moment. Since experiencing this healing work, I've experienced unprecedented personal growth. The catalyst was learning to love myself unconditionally, and to look within for guidance.

The world can become chaotic, and quite frankly terrifying when you can't trust yourself for love, guidance and nurturing. Everything has changed since I've done this. My marriage has become stronger, I am a more present and loving mother, and the cycle of barely getting by has turned into a stream of abundance. And in the process, I've come to understand on the deepest level, that my true purpose in life is to guide my fellow sisters and brothers into this exact space of love. Of knowing themselves, trusting themselves, and loving themselves unconditionally.

KIRSTIE DEMPSEY

Kirstie Dempsey is a mom, wife, and an earth angel, here to guide her fellow sisters and brothers into the light of love. Kirstie resides in Los Angeles and spends much of her time with her son Louis, on the beach, and practicing various forms of meditation, Kundalini yoga and crystal healing. Kirstie is a Reiki Master, a Transformational Image Stylist and brings her passion for energetic healing into her work by guiding women entrepreneurs to step into the power to become the biggest, boldest version of themselves. Learn more at www.kirstiedempsey.com or email info@kirstiedempsey.com.

DEAR 12-YEAR-OLD ME

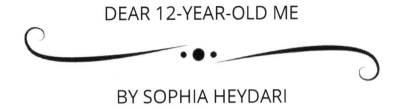

BY SOPHIA HEYDARI

Dear Sophia, I love you. I have a few words I need you to know. There is no shame in trying to take your own life. At twelve years old, you are protecting yourself by attempting to end the isolation. No one to hug, no one to trust, no one to love you back. I see the fear and loneliness in your eyes.

Behind the façade, there lives a loving, compassionate, giving, and fun girl. You were influenced to grow up quickly and convinced that life is hard and people are bad. I wish I could show you that none of this is true. There is no failure because you did not succeed. The truth is, you were not spared, as you believe. You are precious, you are priceless, you are the magnificent light of God. That is why you live. There is so much more for you. Just wait and see little one. Your life is more beautiful than you can ever imagine!

Thank you for your brilliance in hearing His words, "there is more for you" at your darkest moment. Thank you for hanging on to those words when you wanted to make a second attempt. Thank you for trusting yourself at that time.

I forgive you for wanting their love so badly and I forgive

them for not knowing what you needed. Their actions are not a reflection of you. Over the years, you will learn to trust this truth and recognize that love begins within. Only then, can it be given and outwardly received.

I wish I could promise that life gets easier, but it does not. There are more bumpy roads ahead, but with every bump you become stronger and more determined to find the peace and love within yourself. I can assure you that you keep your faith in the words "there is more for you" and you accomplish so many of your heart's deepest desires. You experience confidence and independence upon leaving home at eighteen. You know love at first sight at nineteen. You marry the most gorgeous soul you'll ever know at twenty. You accomplish a first in your family by receiving a bachelor's degree at twenty-seven. You indulge in the selflessness and unconditional love of motherhood at twenty-seven. As you write this letter at thirty-two, you're connecting with your true self. Your forever dream of being happy is fulfilled at last, and you know who you are.

The most important thing to take away from this letter, Sophia, is that you do finally get what you want so desperately. Your parents love and admire you deeply. You are acknowledged and never alone. They see you and know your worth. You make them so very proud.

Today I stand, not as an average mother, wife, and

daughter, but as an empowered woman. I am ready to serve everyone inspired to heal upon reading this letter. It is my intention to bring awareness to the burden and devastation that surviving suicide carries. And to give light to life's possibilities for those contemplating ending their life. Life is a gift worth fighting for. Don't shelter your light, be free.

With eternal gratitude, Sophia.

SOPHIA HEYDARI

Sophia is a soul-truth seeking enthusiast, mother, wife, and daughter. Sophia's passion for self and universal awareness reached a highpoint while studying social work in 2008. She is fascinated with how one's personal inner workings directly affect and are affected by their outside environment. When Sophia is not playing hide-and-seek or hot wheels with her two little boys, she enjoys thought provoking conversation and interactions. She is an avid student of metaphysics and spirituality of all kinds. Learn more by connecting with Sophia at Sophia.heydari@gmail.com.

TO BE RICH IN JOY

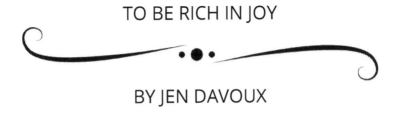

BY JEN DAVOUX

This weekend I finalized my son Austin's senior photos. As I focused through that lens, part of me saw a glimpse of myself, of his dad, and then this fine young man that he has become. Memories flashed through my head of teaching him his first steps, digging in mud, catching frogs, letting go of his hand as he walked into Kindergarten, encouraging him to make a soccer goal, buckling down on him to study for a test and laughing just by hearing his laughter. My heart was overflowing.

Austin is often quiet, shy and always smiles with a grin, but when he has that deep down laughter, his smile shines with those pearly whites. Most of the morning as we captured photos together, I got his grin, his normal look, but I wanted to capture more of him. So, I told him, "Ok, don't smile, then slowly smile and turn it into a laugh that says ha-ha." Yes, this mom and son had more laughter going on than we did taking pictures! The captures of memories we had together were priceless.

The moments were heartfelt, a deep down soul laughter, where nothing else can captivate your attention, other than the moment directly in front of you. You stare and smile and gleam with pride. You witness the reflection of Christ on his life, and you sense everything is going to be all right. You see that once little baby of yours all grown up, as joy fills your heart and becomes whole. Your eyes fill up with tears as you realize you've done everything you could possibly do to reach this point and cherish these precious moments.

As we walked back to our van, he turned and gave me a side hug, saying, "Thanks Mom, good job." There was my aha moment. His words "Good job." My heart soaked his words in. I may not be receiving a diploma, nor graduating this year, but what I am receiving is the fulfillment that for the last 19 years, I've been blessed to be his Mom, and that my love for him will never end. I didn't become a parent for the money, fame or fortune. I desired to create beautiful moments to pour into, to love and lead with all that I knew how too. I wanted to simply be rich in joy.

Yes, there were some long, endless hours as he awoke in the middle of the night, or sat up late doing homework, but it's so clear that being a Mom is indeed full of joy. I'm full of memories that have been etched on my heart, full of miracles both seen and unseen and all of the must-be-felts. I'm full of lessons taught and lessons learned, growing up and growing out.

I'm inspired by how my strengths led and raised him to become who he is today, yet my weaknesses connected me closer to the Lord when I needed Him most. Christ fulfills and sustains me daily, and my identity as a Mom has become a chapter of my life's story. I was never seeking to raise an empire, I play a role in building a legacy. I'm writing the early chapters, so that each of our children can one day turn the page, pick up the pen and create their own chapters.

I am content with not closing this last chapter yet, but pausing and reflecting. I'm writing and feeling from within as stories are never ending. A new book begins to weave through your heart, your mind and your memories, to ignite hope for the future. Your heart underlines the possibility. Truth resonates a bond that runs deep, the courage to continue, the strength to stand strong, and the beauty to see the inner meaning. You reveal the purpose of life, and create a greater vision for what will become. One person's story can be the exact reason for another's paragraph. Your own personal reflection can be the gift needed to cross the T or dot the i for someone else.

Yes, endings can be new beginnings and it can take time to see the outline for your next chapter. It's a seed from within that's growing into a legacy, deeply rooted in solid ground. It's never how a chapter ends that captures your heart. It's the hope you receive as you flip to the next page to discover what's next. It's the determination and strength you feel within. It's the choosing between picking up a pencil and creating your dreams, or relishing in the season of sitting back and resting while focusing the lens on capturing a new perspective.

Your story will continue on with ink spots, tears shed, torn pages, highlighted memories, beautiful words, miracles and prayers answered, all contained within the pages of a book that will always be there to read and reread forever.

One lovely paragraph can be quite a novel. It's our legacy! For our roots are built upon a strong foundation, each generation turning the page, re-writing history and passing it down. We kneel in mind and spirit, just as the sweet humble generations before us. It's a knowing that you will always have a sense of belonging, that you were created for a purpose. Knowing your sense of self-worth, that you're always guided and that there's everlasting love for you. Great is His faithfulness for He is the ultimate best author that's guiding us in writing our stories, the bibliography of us all.

God radiates within my son. He radiates within me and He radiates within you, because you are a beacon of authenticity with your own voice, your smile and the gentle way about you. May you continue to always increase in all the ways that truly matter.

As I sit here looking over all of our photos, I captured his smile, his grin, and the sparkle in his eyes. They may not be professional photos, but I wouldn't want it any other way because it was our day! What's funny is how I find myself gravitating back to one simple snapshot Austin took from his phone earlier this year. I asked him to get me a small piece of chocolate, and he jokingly texted me a picture of a huge Hershey candy bar asking, "Is this big enough for you, ha!" His face radiated with happiness, his laughter captured exactly who he is, and he filled this Mother's heart. To me, it wasn't the chocolate that caught my attention. It was his sense of love and joy that was expressed.

I am gently reminded that my job as a Mom is never ending, and have gained a new perspective toward a friendship that is becoming. Gratitude floods my heart, joy seeps in and love engulfs this soul of mine. Inside a mother's heart is truly blessed.

JEN DAVOUX

Jen Davoux is an inspirational writer, co-author and speaker. She's the wife of a Pastor, has four children and is a successful business woman, operating an organization with Young Living. She equips families for life-long transformation with nature's gift of wellness using essential oils, tips on abundant health, and obtaining financial freedom. Her mission is helping people "see" and unveils their full potential. Following God is far more valuable than all the riches of the world. She walks beside you to unshackle scars and lies to bring forth the light and hope of your true purpose. Contact Jen: http://yl.pe/48p8 ID: 1500731 or Email: aseedwithin1@hotmail.com.

I GOT YOU

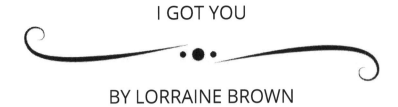

BY LORRAINE BROWN

I'm sitting on my back deck enjoying the cool of the Fall. It's peaceful, a peace that I have always longed for in my life. A robin is resting on a branch and looks my way. I smile, because it feels like God smiling at me. I can see my heart's desires manifesting and I am grateful that I serve a faithful God.

Let me take you back a few years. I was raised in an abusive home where my father lacked loving skills. I didn't know love, recognize it or feel it. I don't fault him as this was how he was raised. But as a result, I grew up not knowing what love is. I married a man just like my father. His parents smothered him because they'd lost their youngest son. He lacked so much in simple life skills, yet I married him knowing his issues. We had three wonderful kids, a girl and then two boys. After seventeen years of marriage, and the night he tried to kill me, I had had enough. I protected our kids and moved to another state. It was important for me to make sure my kids didn't have the same understanding of love as they had seen.

Once we settled into our new place, I was led to place the

kids in therapy, so they could learn healthy ways to deal with anger, disappointment and living in a one parent home. It was difficult, but I knew it was best for my kids and I wanted them to have the best shot possible at life. I prayed a lot. It was the only thing I could do that would calm my heart. I walked in grief. I grieved the loss of my marriage, the loss of what I thought my life should have been. Where was the person I once knew that looked at life with hope and great expectations? What happened to the desires I planned for myself? Where do I go from here?

In time, I grew to engulf myself in raising the kids alone. I worked hard just to keep a roof over our heads at jobs that didn't bring in much income. It was hard at times, very hard. I remember struggling for two years without a winter coat because my priority was making sure the kids were warm. By the grace of God and the determination to raise good kids, I did all that I had to.

I didn't date. I didn't socialize. I focused on the kids alone. I lost myself. I engulfed myself into my kids and nothing else mattered. Somehow, it felt better to focus on them, than to deal with the suffering, loss and feelings of a broken marriage. The one thing that has never wavered, is my trust and faith in God. Sometimes, it was hard to see what was ahead, but we kept moving forward. We took care of each other. My daughter was such a light in my life. She was always encouraging me to keep going and shared often that things will get better. Our bond as a family was unbroken. We went through both the good and the bad, together as a family.

After all of my kids graduated, and my youngest was heading to college, I began to focus on what my goals in life once were, before I got married. What did I want to be when I grew up? That was a hard search. At 50 years old and basically starting again, I was excited to experience life, my life. I was on a quest to find out who I am, and at the same time, enjoying my daughter's pregnancy with her second child. She had so many complications carrying her first child, that I feared we would lose her. Now pregnant again, I feared for her in my heart at times. She was four months pregnant, when she suddenly got sick and went into the hospital with complications. Both my daughter and her unborn child died twelve hours later. I froze. Life stopped. I couldn't breathe. Where was I? How did this happen? God please help me. My only daughter, my best friend, my life coach. It was a hard day. I don't even know how I made it thru those next few days.

Friends, co-workers and relatives surrounded me, yet I felt all alone. I stood at her gravesite and my co-worker's husband placed my arm in his and never left my side. As we walked, I could hear him say "I got you." Later, in the wee hours of the night as I walked the floor crying to ask why, why my child, why Lord? What came to me was "I got you." Over and over I heard the saying "I got you." The voice of my co-worker's husband, became the voice of the Lord, with the assurance of Him carrying me to the next level of my life.

On the 30th day anniversary of her death, I sent Star Jones an email about a fun conversation I had had with my daughter Alicia before her death. Star wrote me right back with kind words. I soon received an email from the producers at ABC who asked me to be a guest on the show. At the time, Star did a "Heart to Heart" segment and she said my story touched her heart. A few weeks later, I was on a plane to be on "The View." Even though it was only six weeks after her death, ABC took great care of me. They even had a Dr. on standby for me if I needed anything. It was an amazing show. They aired it on Thanksgiving Day because that was Alicia's birthday. I now know that God gave me a worldly platform to say goodbye to my daughter.

Four months following her death, I was diagnosed with breast cancer. It amazes me how stress, unforgiveness and worry, can settle into your body in such a negative way. I was fine after an operation to remove the tumor and radiation. Once again, it was God to my rescue saying "I got you."

Although it has been several years since her death, I have spent the last few years growing into who I really am. I'm opening myself up to discover the gifts I've been given. Although I am not married, yet, I am excited to learn more about me. I am healing from old hurts and pain, and replacing them with love.

One positive change that I have made, is to lose some of the extra weight I've been carrying around for years. So far, I have lost almost 40 pounds. As I embrace my senior years, I still want to be able to travel this land and do some of the things I have always desired to do. I want to zip-line, rock climb, inside sky-dive and so much more. I've had to tell myself, "it is not too late, Lorraine." With this, gaining control of my heath is important to me.

One of my desires I had when I was married, was to own our own home. I was raised in a home with land to play on, and that was what I wanted for our kids. My husband did not want the responsibility of a home so that never happened. However, in 2008, I purchased my first home. It's a beautiful home and just what I had always wanted. My desire came true. I held that desire close in my heart for years. By the time I finally got my home, though, I was alone. Both of my sons were busy living their own lives. But, that didn't prevent me from enjoying it. I love to decorate and have seven containers of Christmas decorations alone. My four grandkids keep me busy with crafting and I enjoy teaching them how to cook.

I am now deciding to release my dream home for the next homeowners to enjoy. It took some soul searching to let it go. However, as a result of selling my home, I'm being placed into a much better financial situation that will enable me to do more of what my heart desires. I believe with all my heart God knew that, and the selling of this home will make it possible for me to be able to move forward in comfort.

After working for several years as an Executive Administrator to a General Manager of two Hilton Hotels, I've retired from that and am now taking courses to enable me to help others. My desires are to help heal the land, one person at a time. I have always loved working with people and now I have the time.

As I am learning who I am and what I want to do when I grow up, I find many doors of learning opening up to me. My hearts says, "this feels good." Remember that no matter where we find ourselves in life, be open to learn, grow and love, because it's true that things are going to get easier. I'm always reminded of the most powerful words in my life, "I got you."

LORRAINE BROWN

My hands and heart are full of life when I'm with my grandchildren. If you're struggling, it is my desire to help anyone that needs to move forward in their life. Healing from our past is so important. By understanding where we have been and what we have been through, makes it easier to confront those hurts or pains to move them out of our life. This will enable us to live a life free from the past and walk boldly into our future. I invite you to email me for support or coaching at LorrainBrown@yahoo.com.

ABANDONED BUT LOVED

BY CYNTHIA WASHINGTON

There was a knock at the front door. I opened the door. A very pretty woman with sandy brown hair was sitting in a wheelchair smiling. Her complexion was light. The lady said, "I'm your mother." I was only four years old. Quickly, I turned around, and ran to get my father, who I call Webster. Webster was shaving. His shaving cream smelled like boiled eggs to me. The lady told Webster, "I've came to get my baby." Webster frowned and yelled, "Not over my dead body." Webster closed the door and began telling me not to open the door, when I don't know who is there. His Mother asked him, "Why didn't you let Billie take her baby?" Webster replied, "If Billie wanted her, she would not have left her."

My grandma babysat for my first cousins. One day my cousin told me, "Grandma is not your Mama, so why do you call her Mama?" I never called her Mama again and began calling her Grandma. Grandma and I went to Church often, and when she couldn't attend, she would ask family members to pick me up for church. Grandma always told me, "You reap what you sow and it's better to give than receive." Grandma was sharing

God's words with me all those years.

Webster would take me to my other grandmother's house to spend time with my two older sisters. We bonded closely during these fun times together. On several occasions, I spent the night with my cousin and went places with her family. I used to think to myself, "When I grow up, I will have my own family too."

When I was thirteen years old, I went to live with my mother temporarily, who had remarried years earlier. I got to meet my younger three sisters and one brother. After a few months, I moved back home with my grandma. I decided to attend North High School as that's the school my sisters also attended, along with a few of my friends.

A few years later, I went to a Natalie Cole concert one night. My uncle had dropped me off and told me to call him afterwards. I called him, but no one answered. I began to walk home when a car with three men stopped me. The driver asked me, "Do you want a ride?" I had seen the driver at my sister's apartment, with a friend of hers. Although, I had second thoughts, I got into the car as I felt it was my only option. Have you ever had second thoughts before doing something before? He raped me. His two friends also joined in and sexually assaulted me. The pain was excruciating. I begged God to let me die.

The rapists pushed me out of the car in front of the Hospital Emergency, as they sped off. The Nurse asked me, "Do you know their names?" I answered, "No." The doctor examined me and said, "Plastic surgery is needed."

After surgery, my uncle and cousin picked me up and then other family members took me to a sexual abuse counselor. The counselor suggested I get a journal to write in. I had nightmares for so many years. During the counseling sessions, the counselor would ask me about my childhood. I told the counselor what my Grandma had shared with me that my mother left me at a babysitter's house and never came back so Webster and Grandma picked me up. I suffered from malnutrition and my other grandparents said they wouldn't take another one of Billie and Webster's babies as they were already taking care of two of their kids.

A few months later, I started going out with friends and got pregnant. I went to Planned Parenthood and was told, "It's not a baby yet, it's just a mass of blood." I had an abortion and took a break for awhile.

Four years later, as I was roller skating, I met a young man with curly hair. He could skate very well. We began to get acquainted, started dating and eventually got engaged. When I found out I was pregnant, I was very excited. During this pregnancy, I spent time visiting with my mother, Billie. She shared stories of childhood abuse from her mother, the abuse from Webster, and that she was so young when she had children.

The morning I gave birth to my firstborn, my sister and Billie were with me. My fiancé arrived later that evening. We married four months later and I was pregnant again in six months. I moved back in to Grandma's house as my marriage was quickly failing. I'm thankful God blessed me with two smart and beautiful daughters.

I started attending church again and dressed my babies up to take them to church with me. While I worked, my daughters attended daycare and I began attending Langston University while living in family housing on campus. Once the school year was over, I was driving to Arizona and we had a flat tire. Suddenly, a man dressed in government clothing and driving in a government vehicle offered to fix the flat tire for us. When he finished replacing the flat tire, I went to get my purse to give him money for helping us, and he was gone. I looked in all directions, but he had disappeared.

A few years later, a tall handsome man working on the roof, smiled and said, "Hi, how are you doing?" I said "Hi, I'm okay." About fifteen minutes later, the same man on the roof was now walking toward me smiling. He had light brown eyes and captivated me. We began a conversation and exchanged phone numbers. A week later he called me and we spent countless hours on the phone talking. He asked me out and of course, I accepted. On our first date, we enjoyed dinner and a live jazz band.

As we dated, my cousin invited me to church and I rededicated my life to Jesus. The Pastor taught God's word in a way that I could understand. As I attended the Single's Ministry classes, I learned I have to love myself, before I can love someone else. (Matthew 6:33) "But, seek ye first the Kingdom of God, and his righteousness; and all these things shall be added unto you." This scripture ministers to me. I learned how important it is to forgive myself and other people. (Matthew 6:14) "For if ye forgive men their trespasses, your heavenly Father will also forgive you."

I continued dating the tall handsome man that I met on the roof. As I began attending church more and reading the bible for myself, I invited him to join me. Then one day, I had a fever and felt terrible. I asked my boyfriend to take me to the doctor and my oldest daughter said, "Mommy you are pregnant."

After the exam, the Dr. said, "You have a urinary tract infection and you are six weeks pregnant." We both looked at each and didn't say a word. While I was carrying my third baby, my grandma went Home to be with the Lord. Grandma raised me and was a Mother to me. We gave her a beautiful Home

Going and I continue to miss her today.

Once my third baby was born, my boyfriend moved into our townhouse with us and we began attending Marriage Enrichment Classes to prepare us for marriage. (Ephesians 5:21) "Submit yourselves unto one another out of reverence for Christ." We were engaged and four years later, I gave birth to my fourth daughter. I told my fiancé' that I love him, but I love God more, so we separated a short while to be celibate for a time as we prepared for marriage. We united in marriage, surrounded by our children, with a small wedding. One year later we had our final daughter. Dreams really do come true, so never give up on your dreams.

Over the years, my husband and I have shared some difficult times but I remember that, "it's not who's right, it's what's right." A marriage is not each person giving fifty percent, it's each person giving a hundred percent.

I've always wanted to give my children more than what I endured, and am proud to share that my oldest two daughters have graduated from Langston University with Master's degrees. Our third daughter has received her Associate's Degree. Our fourth daughter is graduating from High School this May and will receive her Medical Assistant Certificate, and attend college. I'm so very proud of all of my children and I'm proud of how far I've come. Dare to **dream boldly**.

CYNTHIA WASHINGTON

Cynthia Washington is a Minister in Training on a mission to expand her knowledge in the Word of God, while encouraging and motivating others to learn the attributes of a Christian life. She's a Youth Ministry Teacher at International Church of the Nations and has been a missionary at Pilgrim Rest Baptist Church. She's the president of the South Minister Headstart Program with thirty six years of parenting. When she isn't sharing God's word, she enjoys spending time cooking, gardening, and taking walks. Connect with her at CynthiaWashington@yahoo.com or WomanOfFaith5@q.com.

SETTING MYSELF FREE

BY NISHA WILLIAMS

I was a young girl born in 1974 to beautiful parents, who are still married today. I have two siblings that are younger than me. I am a very warm, respectful, loyal, friendly, funny, and oh so generous gal, who struggles with her thoughts and has difficulties trying to define who I am. I give so much of myself that I often lose myself in the process. While I grew up in a happy household, I wasn't happy within. I always felt like there was something missing inside of me. Love was all around me, but I was unable to feel it inside of me. I often asked the question, "What's missing?" For the first twenty years of my life, I couldn't feel happy.

One thing I have learned, is that I worry entirely too much about not being loved. I worry about struggling, because of the consequences for the bad choices I made in my past. Everyone has issues in life, but I often feel that mine overpower me at times. We all desire instant gratification, but realistically that's not possible. You get to decide for yourself what's best for you and travel through life making decisions. Those decisions can either make you or break you. Life. It is what you make it. Just like a box of assorted chocolates, every single bite can be completely different.

In past relationships, I gave everything that I had. I thought that's how it was done. I thought having children would give me what I was looking for, but it didn't. I was looking for love in all the wrong places. The heartache and abuse got so great, I wanted to end it all. I drank every single day to the point of being inebriated, to dull the pain I felt from the trauma that was embedded inside.

It was February 2013. I had just gotten off work to go pick up my baby girl from her father's house. It had been a long day, arguing with children and staff, and I just wanted to go home and relax while enjoying some time with my boo. I knocked on his door and he let me in, locking the door behind me. Something felt wrong. He said the baby was sleeping and as he went upstairs to get her, I unlocked the door and cracked it open for an easy exit. I wasn't trusting him one bit and surveyed the room.

He looked back from the top of the stairs and asked me to close the door. I told him to just get the baby as I didn't have time for this. He told me he'd get her as soon as I closed his damn door. I proceeded to walk out and was ready to leave her there, as I couldn't take any more arguing. I said, "Well, I'll stand outside until you bring her downstairs because I don't trust your ass and I'm not standing in this house waiting for you." I closed the door behind me and shook my head in disgust. Meanwhile, my boyfriend was sitting in the car waiting for us, looking at me trying to figure out what's going on.

The door opens and he comes out with my baby. As I take her from his arms I asked where her hat was, as she had it on when I dropped her off. He said, "Look, I don't have her hat. I don't know where it is." I said "You know what, don't even worry about it because you are just ridiculous."

He pulled out a gun and pointed it in my face and said, "What did you say? Yeah, go ahead and put her in the car before I shoot your ass!" I called him a scumbag as the gun was pointing at me while shielding my baby in my arms.

My boyfriend jumps out of the car, walks over to me and said, "Come on baby, put the baby in the car, she doesn't need to see this right now." He then turned to my daughter's father and mentioned he was a clown and had he never been taught that if you pull a gun on someone, you're supposed to use it. I'll spare you the details, but a full on fight erupted, they wrestled around on the ground and when the gun fell out of his hand, they both scuffled to get it, but I ran over, kicked it out of the way and then kicked him in his face. There was blood everywhere. Through the entire ordeal, I couldn't believe my baby was still in the back seat sleeping peacefully.

Police arrived and took statements from me, my boyfriend and my daughter's father. They arrested her father for pulling a gun on me and my daughter, and charged him with two counts of assault with a deadly weapon. They didn't charge me or my boyfriend as he was defending me and my daughter. As I wrote a statement for the police report, I was so upset, shaking, trembling, and crying. I just could not get myself together. The officer walked up and asked me if I was okay. I said I was not. I just didn't know why this had to happen. The relationship we had was up and down, but I never feared for my life in this way. It is hard to imagine that someone can become so in love with a person that they would eventually bring themselves to want to harm them in the most deadly way. Was that love?

I eventually discovered that I needed to love myself first. I turned to God often because He knows best. He will give you everything you need when He sees fit. I know I don't always like to deal with or hear that. I want it on my time, not God's time. It took me awhile to turn to God during times of need, but lately, I turn to Him for all things. I still feel overwhelmed a lot of times, but I'm a work in progress. Aren't we all?

Close the door behind you, lock it, and throw away the key. There's no need to hide in a closet or to feel trapped in your past. Everyone has history. It is His story and God put you here for a reason for you to tell your story, to learn the lessons you're intended to learn, and to be a teacher for others traveling on the path behind you. Accept responsibility for creating your own love and happiness from within, as it makes receiving it, that much sweeter! We continue to grow and sprout like a flowering bulb in the ground. As it cracks open to stay alive, it needs water, nutrients and love. In time though, it turns into a beautiful tulip.

NISHA WILLIAMS

Nisha is an empowerment and positive psychology coach, a writer, a mother who wears many hats and a home-based business owner. Her key philosophy to becoming shame free is choosing to change your perspective. When you do, you begin to change your composure. As you choose to focus more on what God has done for you, than on what others have done or said, you will endure the faith to stand up and press forward. Connect with Nisha at www.icoach4uservices.com or email at bhomewitme@gmail.com.

MY DREAM IS LIKE A LOTUS

BY MEETA GUPTA

Inspirational Dynamo! Yes, this is what some of my friends call me. However, I often wondered if this was a positive exclamation at all. I'm about to share the story of how I transformed radically from ordinary to Supergirl.

In this life's journey, I have learned that there exists a beautiful world inside all of us. When we nourish and connect to this inner space, nothing is impossible. I've learned to fly high up into the inner realms of the sky and to befriend the moon, sun, nature and all of creation.

Once upon a time, I was a young girl with low self-esteem and less confidence. With layers and layers and layers of conditioning and beliefs, based upon my heritage, I became a woman with strong embedded patterns. I was raised in a traditional Marwari Indian family and was never encouraged to pursue any career. I had thus developed a strong belief that being extraordinarily beautiful was the best way to become successful and live a gorgeous life. Though I was reasonably nice-looking, I put forth a lot of effort to look perfect.

Thoughts of imperfection and self-criticism pervaded my mind. I did what others expected me to do, only to make myself feel more accepted. However, none of this made me happy, as I wasn't able to express my true self. Quite the contrary, as I felt like a puppet, performing to make others happy, even at the cost of my own comforts.

After my marriage, I was blessed with a daughter. I was living an ordinary life, yet yearning for extraordinary. I was also raised to believe that my family couldn't be whole or blessed, until I gave birth to a baby boy. I prayed a lot and even consulted astrologers, so that this hope could be fulfilled. I conceived for the second time and wanted a boy. However, I was again destined to give birth to another daughter. Imagine how I felt! After she was born, it seemed to me that I failed, because everyone expected it to be a baby boy.

This added to my suppressed emotions from my past and was too much for me to handle. The thought of conceiving for a third time was overwhelming, adding mental pressure. My mind was filled with confusion, frustration and helplessness. An emphatic question kept haunting my mind. What is the purpose of my life? My self-esteem continued to decline.

I've heard it been said, that when all doors around you appear to be closed, you must look up! I desperately wanted to communicate with the divine, to ask why my life was in such a mess. Then, like a restless honeybee in search of nectar, I started moving from one flower to another. I sought the guidance of enlightened people. Inside, I only wanted to connect with the divine. I was willing to learn new ways and started reading books. This indeed brought solace and peace. I became more aware of my thoughts. I discovered that my dominating thoughts were fear, anger and self-criticism. Books and Coaches helped me to learn how to love myself. For the first time in my life, I learned to focus on what would make me happy and joyful.

I learned how to swim and found that floating on the water and looking toward the sky would give me true pleasure. For the first time, I seemed to embrace my own femininity. This wonderful awareness made me completely change my feelings for my second daughter and I realized what a beautiful blessing she was in my life. I started practicing meditation regularly. It was far from easy and initially it was kind of a compulsive discipline. My mind would throw tantrums and would make up excuses, but soon I found my joy in meditation.

The periods of meditation came to be the most beautiful time of my day. I learned to enjoy my calm, peaceful body with silent rhythm of breath. There was another graceful learning period, once I discovered it is important to enjoy whatever you are doing. It seemed to be a divine sign that I am indeed on the right track. Steadily, the love I felt for myself started spilling over every other creation. My thoughts became bigger. I wanted to connect with the whole Universe. I saw my physical body transforming. I became very energetic. I ascended into practicing advanced yoga. All of this gave me a great sense of fulfillment.

With continuous meditation, I could feel my inner presence. It is a beautiful feeling. This divine, blissful energy is present in all creation, which is not limited to physical body. This energy is omni-present. We just need to connect to it. During our setbacks and challenges, we tend to block the circulation of this energy. However, we can develop a habit of remaining more aware often. In order to develop this habit, you must try to remain aware of what is going on inside the mind and body. Initially, it was just like balancing a bicycle. I would keep falling out to the external world repeatedly. I enjoyed the music of silence, sitting inside the heart of my own being. As I learned to nourish my inner world with my awareness, I continued expanding and reaching further into the Universe. Sometimes I felt as though I was merging with Earth, hugging a tree or sending love to the animals. My soul would feel like I was flying out to the sky to befriend the stars and moon. Nature seemed to unfold her hidden beauties and communicate with me in an inexplicable manner. I felt like a child again to whom those fairy tales no longer seemed utopia. I wanted to embrace my spiritual parents, God and Mother Nature. Now, I truly understand why our spiritual masters said we are all connected. Whenever I witness someone in distress, I have the inner urge to inspire and empower them, by making them aware of their own inner power. My friends call on me in their problems. I love listening to them and inspiring them to experience their **self** and find solutions from the ever so kind Universe.

One day, an idea came knocking on my door. It was the inspiration to write a book to help others discover their inner potential. While I have had no writing background, the very thought of writing a book makes my heart sing. Soon, I began witnessing a series of coincidences happening around me to support and encourage me towards my new found dream. I met people who can coach and guide me on this writing adventure. Whenever I began to feel a little low and considered dropping this apparently formidable dream, things would take some unexpected new turns and I would eventually bring myself back to my writing aspiration. Recently, while I was clearing up the old clutter from my cupboard, I came across a book that I bought during my school years. The name of the book is "Chicken Soup for the Writer's Soul." This added to my inspiration and was another signal from the Divine to ensure my success.

What are the wonderful ways that the Divine is guiding you to **dream boldly**? To live beautifully, we need to let go of our old beliefs and conditioning. We are two-world citizens. Trust your inner voice as it guides you accurately.

MEETA GUPTA

My dream of being a writer was hidden within my heart since childhood. Surrounded by so many constraints, challenges, doubts and mental blocks, I never allowed this dormant dream to flourish. It was only when I started nurturing my inner world, the real purpose of my life became clear. My life is a beautiful adventure and I feel blessed in every moment. My dream is to inspire as many people as I can through my writing. I would love to see humanity realize their inner worth and ascending to higher love. My dream is like a lotus flower, emerging from toils, turmoil and turbulences with flying colors. Learn more at MeetaGupta.com.

MY DREAM, MY LIFE

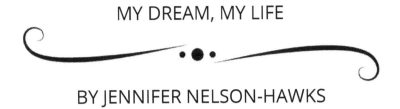

BY JENNIFER NELSON-HAWKS

I remember sitting on my Grandma's lap when I was around nine years old asking her what she did for work when my mom was young. "Well Pumpkin", as she called me, "I was a nurse. I worked in hospitals helping people feel better." "Grandma, that's what I want to do when I grow up! I will be just like you", I said.

The following year, my little sister was born. The only problem was, she was born three and one-half months early. She was so small she fit into the palm of my mother's hand. She weighed one pound twelve ounces, she couldn't breathe on her own and she was not fully developed; but she was a little bundle of joy even though she had tubes sticking out everywhere. You see, five years prior, my mother gave birth to another baby girl that didn't survive, being born three months premature. The thought of losing another sister was heartbreaking for me to even think of. I remembered what my Grandmother said about being a nurse, so I decided I wanted to learn everything about what the nurses did for my sister. I learned how to adjust

135

oxygen levels, shut off heart monitors, and even how to perform CPR on neonatal babies.

When I graduated High School, I was in love! I had been dating the same boy for four years of high school. What am I going to do with my life, I thought? My parents were pushing me to attend college, but the thought of four more years of school without the possibility of being with my love was daunting, as it can be when you are young. I decided to spend the next two years in my hometown attending a technical college to learn the skills I needed to be a Certified Medical Assistant, as I promised my parents I would do. It was the closest I was willing to get at the time to being a nurse without giving up time and my dreams to be with my man.

Shortly thereafter, I received my degree and married the love of my life, the man who would support me through thick and thin, for better or worse. The next five years were great. We traveled, moved, and I supported him in his career changes. The excitement of our ever changing lives was amazing until one day, as we were sitting at the dinner table, he looked up at me and said "I think we have grown apart and I want a divorce." I was twenty-five and the sound of his voice echoed through my body with shards of pain. What, how could this be? How could my life as I know it be over just like this? Tears streamed down my face and I said, "okay" without a single fighting word. What is wrong with me, I thought? My husband just asked me for a divorce and I said "okay".

I drove to my parents' house, numb as could be. When I walked in, my dad was standing there with open arms and I remember collapsing into him with dead body weight as I began to sob! "It's okay my sweetheart", he said. "You will be fine, we will help you get back on your feet and you can go live the rest of your life." In my mind, my life, hopes and dreams were over.

Shortly after the divorce, I decided to leave the small town, so that I could free myself from the constant reminders of my married life. I slowly pulled myself back together to create "my" dream, "my" life! About five years later, I took an opportunity to travel to South America. It was so scary to think about traveling abroad by myself, because it wasn't part of my upbringing. I pulled all my savings together and bought my plane ticket.

When I arrived in South America, a few friends greeted me. I met a new friend on my adventure that happened to live in the same town I did, worked two blocks from where I worked, and was so much fun! We spent the next forty-eight hours being inseparable! I remember the feeling when our arms touched for the first time. It was a spark of cosmic energy that could light up a dark room. What was this feeling and what was happening to me? We arrived home from South America and decided to take on the world. Yes, it was that fast! I knew instantly that he was in my path for a reason. Over the next two years, we built our lives together and were married shortly thereafter.

I felt as if my life was complete. I worked for a physician, which I loved. My marriage was far beyond what I even knew possible. I became an instant stepmom and my health was great. What more could I want? Even though my life was complete, I felt as if I was missing something. I knew I needed to help people differently.

I believe in traditional medicine, but something was nudging me to look deeper into alternative health modalities. I decided at the time, to get my Iridology certification. The doctor I worked for was supportive and encouraging. That was, until I received my certification. He soon sat me down and said "I am sorry, but I feel as if you will be competing with me and I really don't believe in Iridology, so I am letting you go." The same feelings I had at age twenty-five, came rushing over me. My heart sank as the gut wrenching punch to my stomach took hold. I was devastated, completely devastated. How was I going to be able to go home and tell my husband I had been let go from the job I thought I would retire from? I remember him answering his phone on my way home. He praised me with support and all I heard from him was, "sink or swim." I knew there was no option for me to sink! I prayed every day that I was going to be okay and I trusted this was the right path for me. I had no energy, had lost all hope and was questioning my self-confidence.

Two weeks later, I opened my own Iridology office in a small pharmacy. This is where my dreams continue. Over the next four years, I received an abundance of support from my family, my husband, many prayers, listening to my guides and following my heart through intuition. I was on a magical journey to support others in need of guidance and self-healing through many different modalities. In addition to Iridology, I now co-own a pharmaceutical grade supplement store, I perform Bio-Resonance Health Screens, I represent a company named GIA Wellness, I am a Certified Professional Health Coach and currently enrolled in a Holistic Health Physicians Course. My dreams continue to come true every day and as I sit back and take a deep breath, I realize the trials and tribulations were only placed in my way to help me grow and prepare me for this journey, I call life. When you receive that gentle push, dare to **dream boldly** and fly.

JENNIFER NELSON-HAWKS

Jennifer Nelson-Hawks is the proprietor of Peek Purity and Simply Health of Jackson Hole, WY. Upon discovering alternative health care, Jennifer obtained her Iridology certification. She serves on the International Board of Iridology and has completed Bio-Resonance training, Certification as a Professional Health Coach, represents GIA Wellness, and currently Co-owns a pharmaceutical grade supplement store. She creates an exceptional health and wellness experience centered on clients' needs with her compassionate nature, understanding, respect and genuine concern for personalized wellness within. Visit PeekPurity.com, SimplyHealthJH.com or Exploregia.com to learn more about Jennifer's services.

YOUR TRUE SELF

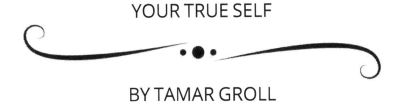

BY TAMAR GROLL

Have you ever noticed that sometimes life just seems to fall into place? The stones of a path just magically appearing before you, leading you on a journey that your true self recognizes. You seemed to have forgotten, although once you take a step forward, you begin to remember and your soul squeals with happiness. All the pieces of the puzzle that you've been trying to fit together, for possibly your whole life, just seem to come together effortlessly. Have you ever experienced this?

It happens so easily once we're aligned with high vibration, but it also happens during those times when we are in the dark night of our soul. When we finally decide that things need to change. When we're ready to change our life and ready to take whatever steps are needed. It's in these moments that we can see some of the biggest shifts in consciousness, our greatest lessons and some of the most beautiful miracles.

It was during a dark night of my soul that I decided I needed to change my life and I was ready to do whatever it took. I had been living a life of adventure for the past nine years. Adventure sprinkled with hard lessons and heartache that is. I was living in

South Beach, Miami at the time. I had moved there to escape an abusive ex-husband, and to start life over, only to fall into another bad relationship, which ended three years later with me moving to Hawaii for a few months to heal. It's not a bad place to heal if I do say so myself!

I had been on my knees praying, crying and pleading for guidance. My boyfriend had just went to jail for being aggressive with me in public and we just so happened to be right in front of the police. I was feeling broken and lost, knowing deep down that I needed deep healing and that I wouldn't get it while being there, seemingly still living in the middle of it. I dreamt of leaving. I had a deep passion for traveling and for experiencing other cultures and people, and decided that this is exactly what I needed in that moment. I envisioned what it was that I needed, and to my surprise, my dream came true within the week.

A good friend of mine showed up at my house and once I shared my dream with her, she offered me a position working with her company in Hawaii. Awaiting for me was a place to stay, some work lined up and the plane ticket was included. I accepted this amazing gift with gratitude and flew out a couple days later. This whole experience left me reeling in amazement when I thought about how easily this dream became a reality. How it fell right into my lap once I was clear on what I desired.

I healed in Hawaii for three months and once I came back, I felt like my old self once again. Note that when I say old self, what I mean, is actually just that. My old self was someone who dealt with issues of feeling unworthy, which stemmed from a traumatic childbirth and being adopted. On top of that was a young, naive choice in a husband and marriage of emotional and psychological abuse, which only added to the deep rooted belief that I wasn't good enough. Needless to say, without working on this deeper issue, true healing never actually took place.

In 2010, I took off again and spent a year and a half traveling and living in New Zealand, searching for myself and my higher purpose. I discovered that what I was searching for was self-love and without it I would never feel truly whole. It was a heart stopping, pivotal moment, when I realized I didn't love myself. When I realized I couldn't look at myself in the mirror and say "I love you". This brought me to tears as I made a vow to myself that I would do the work, to fall in love with myself, possibly for the first time in my life, and so I did. I worked hard on me. I left my boyfriend, as I realized it wasn't in alignment with who I was and what I wanted, and then I moved back to South Beach.

This is where my story takes a turn for the worse, before the magic happens. As with all things in life that we try to work through, sometimes, well, we just mess up, again and again until we finally get hit in the head with a 2 x 4 (or at least that is how it seems to happen for me). You see, in South Beach, being the wild free spirit that I am and always up for new experiences and having fun, I started to dig myself back into a hole.

What I desired was for my soulmate to appear, to settle down, to have an amazing relationship, to travel the world and to find my purpose in life. I even sat down and made a list of all the qualities that I wanted in a partner, but the list got buried in my notebook while I was flitting around like a butterfly from one thing to another. I was continuing to do a lot of deep self-work, but at the same time I was also running full speed, living the fast life, partying, not sleeping much and working two jobs just to afford to live. I had made a pact with myself to remain single until I learned how to love myself, but continued dating unavailable men, because I was unavailable.

It was the end of 2013, and I again realized I was losing myself. I was losing myself to the full throttle life, and knew that if I didn't get a grip on my life, and soon, that I could really be in trouble. I needed a way out, and fast. As a birthday gift, a friend of mine gave me a cd set on the law of attraction. He had used it himself and knowing that I was spiritually open, he thought I would love it too. It was also around this time that I decided to cut things out of my life that no longer served me, such as friends that brought me down, jobs that didn't align with who I was, and the unavailable men that I kept around. I went through my life and like scissors to paper, I started cutting things away.

The last thing that needed to be cut away took place on New Year's Day. Being too busy to listen to the cd before now, it became my resolution as I entered 2014, to begin this New Year with better decisions. I decided this New Year would be a different year for me and it would begin on the very first day of the year. I listened intently to the words on the cd. It awakened me to the fact that I'd manifested my dreams into reality before, but I hadn't understood what I was actually doing.

Knowing that it worked, I spent every day working on it, envisioning what it was that my heart truly desired and releasing everything else that I no longer needed. I spent an hour a day doing my visioning work. I was intent on changing my life and it was going to begin now. I envisioned every part of the life I dreamed of: the husband, the child, working with my life purpose, traveling, feelings I wanted to feel, everything. I decided and declared to my best friend that I would move to Paris in April of that year and I would meet my husband there. Why would I say this? Now I know it was my higher self, my intuition, guidance from spirit, that placed these thoughts into my mind. I had finally gotten clear on what I wanted and I started living only from a high vibration of joy. Once I did that, it opened the door for Spirit to start working.

Two weeks later, my soulmate showed up in such an unexpected way and guess where he was from? France! Not Paris, but he was in France of all places, and actually as much as I love Paris, I now realize the French Alps are a much better location for me at this point in my life. It was my best friend that introduced us. When I told her I had made the decision to move, she knew it was the perfect time to introduce me to her French cousin. Within three days, I knew he was the man I was meant to be with.

Can you believe that the dreams I had envisioned, the words I had used in my visioning, were some of the exact words that he used to describe things to me? Needless to say, I moved to France in July, only three months later than I had envisioned. We were married first in France on December 31, 2014. One year, almost to the date, that I started dreaming my life into being. We married again in the US on July 31, 2015. It was during this trip to the US that I rediscovered my notebook from early 2013 stating all of the qualities that I wanted in my partner. As I reread it, tears started pouring almost to the point that I could no longer see the paper clearly. If you can believe that everything I had written, all of the qualities that I had wanted in a husband, is exactly what I received! It is now our two year wedding anniversary, and I'm still in shock when I think about it, as I consider what happens once we actually get clear and declare our dreams.

I now understand my life's purpose and am building my business around it, helping other women heal deep emotional wounds and to find true love within themselves. To also help them learn to bring their true hearts desires into being and to find the magic in the everyday. This has allowed me to take everything that I have learned and gained, and turn it into something beautiful to share with the world. Each of you can do the same. You can create the life you've always dreamed of. It is more than possible. I am living proof. Don't just dream, **dream boldly**!

TAMAR GROLL

Tamar is a shamanic midwife, working with women to reconnect with the ancient wisdom within them, to recognize their sacredness, thus healing the divine feminine. She mentors women in reconnecting to their wild feminine archetype through her online courses and her sacred online sisterhood temple. She is also a holistic transformational coach guiding women one on one to find their truth, voice and personal power in order to create fulfilling relationships, reconnect to their sensuality and live a life they are passionate about. She conducts retreats world-wide as well as courses and workshops both online and in person. Learn more at www.TamarGail.com.

HEALTHY AS YOU ARE

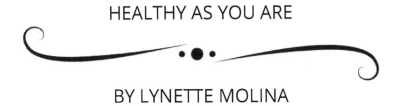

BY LYNETTE MOLINA

I've been small, medium, large and x-large on my 5'2" frame. I've been healthy and unhealthy, but I've never really felt pretty. I have attempted all of the diets. You know the ones I'm talking about; cabbage soup, Slim Fast, South Beach, Atkins, not to mention Richard Simmons and Denise Austin VHS tapes. I was coke and my family is water. I am donuts and they are green juice.

I struggled with my weight for years and finally had enough! No more diets. No more starting on Monday. No more joining gyms and never going. What changed? My mindset changed! When you change your thoughts, you change your life. The struggle ends when we end it. I lost 68 pounds. I can share with you that it wasn't easy, but it has been worth it! I began believing I was worth it and that I didn't need to be skinny. I wanted to be healthy! I wanted to set an example for my two daughters. I started taking better care of me.

Fall in love with taking care of you! Love yourself so you can fully love others. Give up the diets, enjoy the donuts and celebrate the wine! It's a lifestyle! Make lots and lots of small choices daily to drink more water, eat less crap, eat more veggies, and move more! Enjoy walking, dancing, yoga and hiking, as fitness can be fun. Don't go to the "gym" if it's not your thing. Find your fitness happy place!

Today, I'm 54 and I just finished training to be a yoga instructor. It was one of the hardest things I've ever done. Now, I'm eager to attempt pickleball! I don't even know what it is, but I am willing to try it. It's never too late to start your healthy lifestyle. Don't wait for New Years to make a resolution. You can make a declaration anytime, to start a season of healthy living. I have a passion for empowering people with love, support, tools and training to equip them in fighting for their success, for their health!

We can age, happy and healthy. It's not all about the number on the scale. Focus on sleeping better, enjoying how your clothes fit, feeling vibrant and looking radiant! And the next time someone asks you how much you weigh, simply reply, one hundred and awesome, because you are!

(1 Cor. 6:19) "Your body is a temple of the Holy Spirit."

LYNETTE MOLINA

Lynette Molina is a yoga teacher and owner of Kingdom Yoga LLC., the founder of Fight for It (a healthy lifestyle support group), a reluctant health nut, and red wine and donut enthusiast. Her passion is encouraging, uplifting, supporting and cheering on friends and family, both new and old. As an empty nester at 54 years young, she believes we're never too old to make our dreams come true. Learn more at LynetteMolina.com.

A HEALING JOURNEY

BY DR. LINDA POTTS

Super Bowl Sunday, January 1998, I dropped to the floor with severe pain stabbing my upper right abdomen.

"If I didn't know better, I'd think I was having a gallbladder attack," I said, but I knew that was unlikely because I didn't eat fried fatty foods. Besides that, for 42 years I had eaten right and exercised, just as I was told I needed to do to stay healthy. I could not imagine what was going on in my body.

"You need to get to the ER," someone suggested. It was a logical idea, but having been an ER/Trauma Nurse for many years, I knew that if I showed up without some sort of trauma happening, I'd be far down the list for diagnosis and treatment. So I decided to wait until morning.

When I arrived in the ER the next morning, miserable and still experiencing severe pain, I was whisked to the radiology department for abdominal x-rays. That done, I sat patiently in a wheelchair wondering what would happen next. Shortly, the radiologist, who was a friend, came up to me and said, "I don't know how you even made it in here, Linda. I don't know what is wrong, but I can tell you that every organ in your body is totally inflamed!"

Well, that was the beginning of a long, long illness, and I went in and out of consciousness for the next three weeks. Then oh-so-slowly over the following months, my health began to improve slightly. Eventually, I was able to get back to work, but I still couldn't do much of anything. My boss even had a cot put in my office so I could lie down and rest, if needed, during the work day.

Over the next four years, I endured lots of testing and visits to many medical specialists. After four years, I had become bedridden and had to quit my job. Specialist after specialist sadly told me they had no idea what was wrong with me or how to help me. Even so, I felt reassured that they believed something was causing all my symptoms, and not that I was just crazy.

I was offered diagnosis after diagnosis, all with life-changing negative considerations. Through the years, I was told that it might be multiple sclerosis, a brain tumor, Chronic Fatigue, Fibromyalgia and Lyme disease.

My family doctor, whom I have great respect for as a person

and a physician, told me, "You may have to just live like this the rest of your life." Bedridden! My immediate response was, "No! That is not an option!"

At that point, I decided to investigate alternative medicine to see if there was something that path could offer toward taking my health back. Thus began another, different journey as I tried acupuncture, chiropractic sessions, and many different herbal supplements of varying credibility. I would feel a little better for a few days, but soon would go right back to my debilitating state. I was frustrated and disappointed time after time. Emotionally, I was drained.

I had many conversations with God as I lay in bed, not able to move without moaning. Not able to walk myself to the bathroom because my feet hurt so much. Not able to feed myself at times because I was in so much pain, I could not hold a fork. I couldn't even carry on a conversation with someone without my husband there to translate what I was trying to say. I would try to say something and the words would come out all jumbled. I would forget words or say the wrong words, thinking I had actually said what I meant to say.

I told God how frustrated I was and how confused I was with the situation. Here I was, fortunate to be well-educated with many skills. I liked working and enjoyed helping people. What did I do to cause this situation? What was I missing? What did I need to do to get well?

Day after day, no change. Week after week, month after month, year after year. No change. Time crept and time flew. Either way, nothing changed. It seemed I always got just a little worse, and worse, and worse. I was so discouraged and desperately wanted to get better.

Even with all these feelings, I was determined to get well. I pictured myself as a healthy person. I tried to hold on to that vision each day. The answer was out there, I knew it. It must be out there somewhere. I just hadn't found it yet.

Then, a friend from church told me I needed to have a particular screening done. By this time, I was exhausted and extremely discouraged, having tried so many things without success. But, I knew I couldn't give up so I went for the screening, and even while I was there, I knew this was my answer. I was given a multitude of supplements to take and two weeks later, I went back to the person that performed my screening and asked, "What do I need to do to learn how to do this testing?"

Because of the significant level of pain in my body, I didn't recognize any improvement for a full six weeks after starting the supplements. Somehow I knew inside of me that this was going to work for me. I believed it, and I did exactly what I was instructed to do.

By month six, I felt like I finally had my life back and I began my own business, performing the same health screening I had been given. I became certified as a BioEnergetic Practitioner and continued my educational journey to learn as much as I could, so I would be able to help others in the same type of situation I had been in.

Never ever did I dream that I would have my own business, but I loved it! Then after two years, my husband began encouraging me to expand my business and offer all the things that helped me get healthy. I was happy working part-time and didn't want to do anything else. At least that's what I kept telling myself. Truthfully, what was going on in my head was that I was scared! I was afraid that if I did more, I would get sick again. If I got sick again, how would I be able to help anyone else or even get anyone to believe me and trust me?

My husband continued encouraging me. He found a building that would work well for creating a Wellness Center. By now, I was terrified. Could I do this? Was it just a crazy idea or was I being led by God?

All this time I was praying and praying. I kept feeling this was what I was supposed to do, but the fear was huge. I could envision the whole thing and during the previous two years, had many conversations about growing the business, but I was thinking way too far into the future. So, I had a serious conversation with God. I made a deal (it's funny how we do that sometimes). I told Him, I would take this one step at a time. If He opened a door, I would walk through it. I was still scared, but now I was determined to keep my word. My husband had found the right building so now it was my job to find the money to make this bold dream happen.

"OK, God, now what?" I asked. I had spent all my savings on trying to get well. I hadn't been employed for quite some time as I was too sick to function and people are typically reluctant to lend money to someone who is self-employed, let alone only part-time.

My next step was to create a business plan and make a plea with the Small Business Administration for a loan. I was trying to convince myself I could do this. After all, I had a Master's degree in Business Administration, yet I was still terrified. I kept thinking, "just take one step at a time."

My first step was to focus on creating a great business plan. As I began working on it, my dreams continued to expand. This was beginning to get exciting! I could envision a healing Wellness

Center with various health practitioners providing their services, with rooms for other modalities to heal people.

Then one day as I was working on the plan, there was an unexpected knock on my door. When I answered, I was surprised to see someone who rarely came to my home. I invited him in, curious as to his surprise visit. He asked what I was doing and I quickly responded, telling him I was working on a business plan to try to get the money I needed to start my full-time business.

Imagine my shock when he offered to back me in obtaining my business loan. My mouth literally dropped open! I couldn't believe my "one next step" had just been completed. After that, everything fell into place as I continued to just take one step at a time. Within a few months, my husband and I remodeled the building and in January 2006, I opened my doors for business.

I am proud to say that I have now been running my successful health practice for 12 years. Over this same period, I earned a Master's degree in Bioenergetics, a Doctorate in Clinical Religious Counseling, a Doctorate in Naturopathy and became Board Certified in Natural Medicine. I still have days when my health is less than optimal. But, after being so ill for so long those many years ago, a day here and there is nothing to complain about at all.

I am so grateful to have performed thousands of health consultations with patients during these years and so happy to have allowed myself the opportunity to dream far beyond what I believed was possible for me. I absolutely love what I do and welcome each day in with excitement as I discover what each new day holds for me.

With this, my message to you is simple. Believe. **Dream boldly**. And never give up! You'll never know what you can do until you give it a try.

DR. LINDA POTTS

Dr. Linda Potts, ND, DCRC, RN, MBA, MBE is the owner of Healing Waters Wellness Center, as well as a Health Care Practitioner and Health Coach, specializing in educating and helping enlightened individuals take control of their health as a whole being; addressing physical, mental, emotional and spiritual aspects. Learn more at HealingWatersWellnessCenter.com or email HealingWaters@myactv.net. Download her free e-book @ https://drlindapotts.leadpages.co/heal-yourself.

WHOLE, HEALTHY AND FREE

BY CHRISTINE RYAN

I remember waking up and realizing I had slept through my birthday and Thanksgiving. I had been asleep for three days (after being awake for five).

It was 2002, and I had moved to Las Vegas after Hollywood seemed to have gone bust after getting a DUI. I thought I was rerouting my life well by moving and getting enrolled in school for massage therapy. Wrong again. Within six months I'd dropped out, got married with a ring pop in a Vegas Wedding Chapel, and was living in a Budget Suites, about to get evicted. I was working as a cocktail waitress at Club Platinum, smoking a pack a day, gambling with my tips and using crystal meth daily. Can anyone say "addictive personality"?

Thankfully, I am one of the lucky ones as this isn't how my story ends. I was blessed to have friends and family that supported me and had strength and faith in me. I owe gratitude to more people than I can count, for where I am today. I chose not to let my worst years define me. That is not my story. That is part of the integral path that led me to my calling and my passion. I embrace my past because it allows me to help others more fully, and I'm able to relate to so many circumstances. It's a testament that all things can be overcome and that the only things that can truly hold you back in life are found in the choices you make. Your choices are not you. Your choices are made up of actions taken. Don't like where you are? Take a new action. Yes, others actions can indeed affect your life. You do have a choice to allow or disallow those actions to gain power over you though. Switch it up! Change your perspective. If you take nothing else away from this, let it be that **you** determine **your** life.

Now, I want to share my new story! I get so excited about this, because it's uplifting, wholesome, healthy and free! It's a complete juxtaposition from my old story, where I was the victim of sexual abuse as a child and let that validate my poor choices. My story, now inspires and empowers others, gives hope and is allowing me to live more fully than ever before, while helping others achieve the results they want in their own lives.

In July 2015, I looked in the mirror and realized I was fatter than I'd been after giving birth four years prior. I was not taking care of myself. I was tired, bitter and fat. I'd tried all the diets. I now realize that nothing worked because I wasn't taking responsibility for my own actions. No one was force feeding me doughnuts and pizza, so I made a decision. I put the right support, system and accountability in place that I needed, so that I could follow through and I lost 40 lbs. in five months. It was awesome! Empowering! It gave me confidence to address other things in my life. My job was next. After five years with State Farm, I resigned on a whim, with no inkling of what would come next. I started googling health, wellness, fitness and the like. I saw an ad for an institute promoting their Health Coaching Certification and I knew without a doubt this was it!

I wanted to share the tools I had put in place to feel balance, and the validation of being present within my own life. I wanted ladies to know that taking care of yourself first allows you to be a better mother, wife and friend. And, I wanted to help others shed unnecessary weight. Not only the physical weight, but all the baggage and skewed perceptions from experiences that no longer serve us. I wanted to share the ability to feel light! Weight loss was where my new story began and I knew it was a doorway to help others re-write their life stories too.

I fully embraced the training and became a certified health coach with a quickly growing business, clients served and well affected with results that exceed their expectations. I totally geek out on anything health and wellness related and have great referral relationships established within my community. I work the schedule that suits me and my family is my #1 priority, which feels amazing! I have a brilliant, fun, loving, beautiful daughter who breaks out in song on a regular basis and asked me for artichokes and mango for dinner last night. I have a passionate, adoring, supportive husband who has also lost 40 lbs. and is excited for my new career and lifestyle changes. I focus on abundance in all that we have to be grateful for each and every day. Life is good.

Today, I sit here typing on my laptop in front of my crackling warm fire on this chilly morning in my home just outside Richmond, VA. It's a beautiful, affluent neighborhood in an excellent school district where most people would likely be shocked and appalled at my backstory. That's okay. The people that matter don't mind, and the people that mind don't matter. I am happier than I have ever been and I know that this is my beginning. My journey is here and now, the best is yet to come and this is my story. I am 36 years young, wide awake and ready to serve at my highest capacity.

CHRISTINE RYAN

Christine Ryan is a wife, mother, Certified Health Coach and owner of Weight No More Health Coaching. In her business she helps busy moms create sustainable habit changes to reach their goals while dropping excess weight. She loves to cook and eat, and has recently started a blog to share delicious recipes and tips to encourage and support a well-nourished, healthy lifestyle. Learn more at WeightNoMoreHealthCoaching.com.

POWER IN YOUR STORY

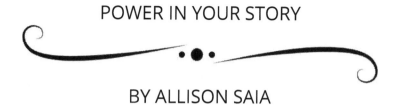

BY ALLISON SAIA

I was 21 years old and sitting on the cold steel of an exam table wearing only a paper gown and thinking, "My life is ruined. He's going to walk in and tell me my life is over." And he did, but it wasn't. My life was only beginning and the beginning of my life started with the beginning of another's. The journey from there to where I am now was a roller coaster ride of finding myself and finally stepping into the person I was meant to be.

I had my whole life planned since I was young. I would go to college to be a criminal psychologist, become an FBI agent, and live out my life single and childless. But, here I was a junior English major in college and pregnant to a guy I had only known for three months while studying abroad in England. Running was what I always did best. And deciding to spend my Junior year of college in England was a prime example of that. When people got too close, I'd run. I'd run because I didn't want them to really know me, because the truth was I didn't know myself.

Since I was a child I had suffered from depression, which I never understood. I just knew I was different from the other kids. I suffered in silence. The only thing that ever brought me comfort was the written word. I wrote poem after poem about how I felt. I had various journals filled with essays and thoughts. The sadness and pain was so much easier to deal with when I put ink to paper. It was like all the bad stuff poured out of me with each drop of ink.

I went to college and had a successful freshman year, until I was sexually assaulted on the last night of Spring semester. That threw me into a tailspin. I won't go into the gory details, because that part of my life isn't what this story is about. I fell in with the wrong crowd and drowned myself in sex, drugs, and alcohol. I knew if I kept on going that way, I wouldn't end up seeing 22, so I decided to do what I always did and I ran all the way to Ormskirk, England. It was there that I met the father of my son and ended up on that cold table one day in January of 1994.

When I say that I thought my life was over, it is not an exaggeration. I was devastated. I had no desire to be a mother and didn't think I even had the strength to try. At the same time, part of me was desperate for roots, desperate for something to hang onto and this was my shot. So, my boyfriend moved to the United States and in August of 1994, I became a mom. What a foreign word to me! What did it even mean? It was a label I never thought I would have.

I got married two months later and we started our young little family. Being a mom wasn't as difficult as I thought it would be, but feeling like a mom was a different story. I struggled to find myself amongst the diapers and the tears. I loved my son beyond all comprehension, but I wasn't loving myself. I felt like a failure every single day and I mourned for the person I wanted to be. I never felt good enough for my son or for my husband. I never felt good enough for anything. I wouldn't, couldn't, even look myself in the mirror because I had no idea who the person was that was looking back.

Three years went by and my heart expanded a bit more when my second son was born in 1997. While my capacity for love expanded exponentially, my capacity to feel love and love myself melted into oblivion. I poured every ounce of myself into my boys and was left with nothing for me. It went far beyond just being lost, so I confided in my doctor. I was formally diagnosed with depression and was put on antidepressants. I started to feel like myself again and enrolled in a local college to finish my degree. So, with two children under the age of 5, I went back to school full-time. And in two years, I graduated with Honors with a B.A. in English/Creative Writing.

I felt like I was finally getting myself back. But, I still felt broken somehow. I felt lost without a voice or a purpose. I felt like a shell of a woman. I was homeschooling two amazing sons, finally had my college degree, but the hole remained. That black hole just engulfed me a little bit every single day. And I didn't know why. I could feel happiness, but I wasn't happy. For years, I struggled with who I was and who I wanted to be. I defined myself based on the people in my life: mother, wife, daughter. But, I never knew who I was. I loved my sons more than life, but something just wasn't right inside me.

Time moved on and my marriage became more and more turbulent every day. I admit, I was very difficult to live with and my husband took the brunt of my frustration, loneliness, and despair. There were daily fights and financial struggles. Our house became toxic to us and to our children.

It's so hard to describe into words what those years felt like. I chose to live for my sons. I gave every ounce of me to them and their education, and I put myself on the backburner. My degree hung on the wall, but that's all it did. This went on for almost 16 years until my husband couldn't take it anymore and left. I was relieved and scared at the same time. Although my marriage wasn't happy, it was stable and secure and gave me a place to hide away from the world and from myself. When he made the decision to leave, it was a wake-up call that I needed to do something, because I only had myself to depend on now. I needed to take care of the woman I was and be strong for my boys. So, I went to a psychiatrist for the first time in my life. It was there that I got some clarity.

She diagnosed me with BPD (Borderline Personality Disorder). It was a scary diagnosis, as people with BPD are portrayed as dangerous psychopaths in the media. But, the more I read up on it, the more I finally understood who I was and why I was. The stigma that still exists on mental illness made me afraid to tell anyone. I read everything I could on my illness and started practicing all the mindfulness techniques to cope with it. The odd thing was even though I was given this frightening reason why I was the way I was, I felt free for the first time in my life. I could fully step into who I was and use it to my advantage. I allowed my mental illness to empower me instead of consume me.

Around the same time that I got my diagnosis, someone unexpected walked into my life. My high school boyfriend from freshman year and I connected on Facebook. It was as if no time had passed. We met for coffee and for the first time in my life, I wasn't scared to be myself with someone. I had made the decision to be totally honest with him from the beginning and he loved me enough to want to understand. He did research on BPD, got advice from BPD support groups, and with his support

I flourished even more. I started writing for the local newspaper and was eventually elected Poet Laureate of my hometown. I felt like a brand-new woman with a purpose.

I started working in publishing and worked my way up to Editorial Director of a publishing company. As I worked with clients that were getting their personal stories out to the world, I noticed how many of them were like I once was. Scared and lonely and unsure of who they were. Their identities were based around their relationships or their careers and the essence of the authentic person inside was lost in the shuffle. It was then that I knew what my life's purpose was. I needed to empower others to fully step into their stories and into their authenticity. So, I started my own coaching company and partnered with colleagues in a publishing company. My soul's purpose is to help others struggling to find their story and empowering them through the writing process to fully embrace who they are and what they were put here to do.

I've come a long way since that day in the doctor's office over 22 years ago. The woman that is here now is a much different person than I thought I would be. It wasn't until I stepped out of all the labels I had put on myself: mom, wife, daughter, BPD sufferer, etc. that I could fully be me. And when I finally met that woman that struggled for so many years to be heard and seen, when I finally looked in the mirror and saw her looking back, I really liked her.

ALLISON SAIA

Allison Saia is the owner of Allison Saia Consulting and co-owner and Editorial Director of Positive Media Press. She prides herself as a professional wordsmith and a highly effective writing coach. With over 25 years of writing and editing experience, Allison brings a wealth of knowledge and expertise to her work. Her passion is helping clients find their voice and guiding them, hand in hand, in their writing journey. When she's not coming up with clever quips, Allison enjoys spending time with her beloved husband, Dan and her two college-aged sons, Holden and Harrison. Learn more about Allison at: www.allisonsaia.com and her publishing company at www.positivemediapress.com.

RAYS OF HARMONY

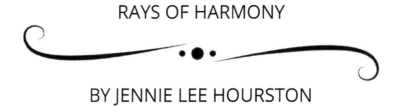

BY JENNIE LEE HOURSTON

Have you ever been at a point in your life where you feel miserable, stuck, and alone with no way out? Have you spent endless nights in tears thinking, "God, why? Why does life have to be so difficult for me?" Do you feel like you need to change everything in your life, because there just isn't any other option, but you have no idea where to even begin or how to make it work? This was me not so long ago.

I was a single parent, living with my pre-teen daughter and commuting over two hours a day to a job that made me feel empty and exhausted. I worked for a large insurance company that had been undergoing some major changes that resulted in restructuring, more work for the same pay and no promise of security for employment. I had started a small cleaning company on the side which taught me the "do's" and "don'ts" of business along with networking, public speaking, presentation and the fine details of dealing with taxes and government requests. To make things just a little more exciting for myself, I was going to school part-time for an accounting course which required exams, studying and a lot of homework.

I felt pulled in over 100 different directions and I was tired, all the time! In the midst of it all, my teenage son was battling severe depression, so he had moved in with my mom at 15 years old. He had expressed early signs of depression since I left my abusive marriage, four years prior. There were many circumstances that occurred during that four-year span, which I feel contributed to his depression. We had lost my stepfather to a blood disorder that caused his organs to slowly shut down and the untimely passing of my uncle who was taken from us far too soon. That was a very difficult time and I was not taking care of myself at all, in any way. This made me feel even less of a mom because I was dealing with so much. I didn't have the energy I needed to guide my children to the capacity they needed me. I could see my son was not happy, yet I was doing everything I thought possible to get him help. I was dealing with meetings and phone calls with teachers at his school, counselors, social workers and doctors.

The doctor wanted to prescribe anti-depressants for him. When I looked into the side effects, I discovered that there are risks that did not seem at all good (may cause suicidal thoughts). I spoke with the doctor about my concerns and we agreed that he would take them for six months at a very small dose. He took them for two weeks and although he seemed happier, he told me he was feeling "numb" and like a "zombie." He expressed to me that the pills were not a good option because they made him feel so out of touch, and I felt torn. I wanted to support his desire to stop taking the medication, but also felt like I needed to side with the doctor. I felt that we needed to deal with the root cause of his depression, rather than just rely only on prescribed medication.

My mother has always been supportive of me and I love her dearly, but when it comes to dealing with my son, we have different ideas of how to try and help him, so we argued a lot about it. When things came crashing down and my son went to live with my mom, I was miserable and felt like a complete failure. Things had to change, and quickly. I started to investigate alternative and natural forms of healing. I came across Reiki, but really had no idea what it was or how it worked, but it caught my interest and I felt a strong "pull" toward it. My long- time best friend from high school called me one day and said "We need a spa day." I will admit, I felt like I was being selfish and irresponsibly spending money on myself to get pampered.

My friend advised me how important it was to take time for myself and that I deserved to have some self-care in my life. We made an appointment for the spa the following weekend. Something magical happened that day! I was actually booked in for a facial treatment and I had asked the woman about Reiki, as I knew they offered the service. I told her I was interested in booking a session as I got settled in for my facial. The woman was circling her fingers around my eyes and I felt a very warm sensation. One I will never forget. She put cotton pads on my eyes and left the room for about five minutes. I started to cry (bawled my eyes out). She came back in and pulled the cotton from my eyes. I said, "I don't know what has come over me. I can't stop crying."

She looked at me gently and said "I could feel the pain in you from the moment I looked at you. The circling motion around your eyes was just a sample of Reiki that you said you wanted to try. I'll finish your facial and then I want you to go home and cry. Let it all out and then come back next week for a full Reiki treatment." She was right. In dealing with the pain of leaving an abusive marriage, working in a job that brought me no joy, running a small business, trying to provide for my kids and feeling like a failure as a mother, I was not even allowing myself to release the pain.

I was desperately trying to be strong for my kids, strong at work to deal with my duties, strong at night to provide dinner and try to help with homework and after school activities. At night, once the house was quiet, I was too exhausted to cry. I went home and did what she said. I cried. I think I cried all day. I went back the following week for a full Reiki treatment. That was the beginning of my huge aha life changing moment. I had two choices. I could continue feeling sorry for myself and stay down and out, or take action. The decision was clear. I was hooked on taking control over my life, rather than having it control me.

It was scary and exciting all at the same time. I worried about how I would find the money, time and energy to chase my dreams. I learned everything I could about Reiki and energy work. I became attuned to level 1 Reiki in 2014 and started to practice as much as I could. I knew in my gut and my heart that this was something I had to share with as many people as possible. I went on to obtain my level 2 Reiki so that I could treat people no matter where they are in the world. In January of 2016, I went for a one day intensive coaching program that truly changed my life for the better. I had worked on self-development and invested in training for mindset, abundance, fears, blocks, decision making skills and finances.

My world awakened to new and wonderful people who are positive, loving and truly genuine in their work of helping others reach their dreams! When I made the decision to invest **big** in myself, my life truly began to shift for the better. I also continued with more energy training. I became certified for Axiatonal Re-Alignment (another form of energy work that goes great with Reiki). I worked with a business coach to see the possibilities of starting my own health and wellness business and learned how to change my mindset from "victim" mode to one of freedom and lessons. I also learned one very big lesson that was a hard one to accept. That lesson is this; as much as we want to "fix" someone we love, we need to respect their decision of allowing and accepting our help, along with the decision not to accept anything we have to offer. The same goes for anyone who chooses to work with me. It is not my job to "fix" someone. It is my calling to guide, offer support, tools and resources to those who want to change.

I am now running a coaching business using my energy work and personal experience to help women find their inner goddess, to create independence for themselves and move past fears and blocks in order to help them live out their dreams! I have found my calling and was shown how we are provided with all we need. You just have to dream, believe and take action!

JENNIE LEE HOURSTON

Jennie Lee is passionate in improving all areas of the body, mind and spirit. Through Reiki, Axiatonal realignment and energy coaching, she helps clear blocks that hold you back from living the life you desire. We all have an energy force in and around us made up of emotional, mental and spiritual particles. Reiki sends positive energy to eliminate blocks that cause illness, stress, and negative thoughts. Ready to take control and let your highest spiritual, emotional and physical being take charge? Receive a consult as my gift to you at JenHourston@gmail.com.

MY LIFE SAVING MOVE

BY KATHY MORTENSON

I had heard people say things like, "People get sick when they are unhappy," and "When your life is out of balance, it creates illness," but those words never really sunk in until a few short years ago. It is a vivid memory imprinted in my mind like it happened yesterday. The year was 2012. It was a hot summer day in Arizona. I was sitting in the corner chair of the only patient room at my doctor's small office. I had just finished working a four-week trial in Los Angeles and had returned home to Phoenix a couple days before. I was physically exhausted from work. My doctor asked me to come in to get some tests done. She came in, we talked and caught up. When the tests were complete, my scores were worse than my last visit. I was disappointed, but not surprised, given the long hours I had worked in Los Angeles while living in a five star hotel. Sounds glamorous, but being away from home and eating hotel food gets old quickly. She sighed, hesitated, then looked me in the eyes and said, "Kathy, if you don't change your career or your lifestyle, you're going to slowly kill yourself. I don't know how else to say it." I just stared back at her. I had no words. I sat there thinking what to say. No words would come out. I think the only thing I said was, "Ok," but that's just a vague recollection. I remember heading out to my car. Then it hit me like a freight train. I sat in my car and the tears started coming, slowly at first, and then all-out gushing. I knew I had to make a change, but I just didn't know what to do or how to do it. The only thing I did know, was that my life depended on it.

Being a trial paralegal is what I had done for over 20 years. Endless deadlines. Crazy hours. Courtroom drama. Food on-the-run. Lots of computer screen time. Texts and emails 24/7. I had always had the energy for it. In fact, sometimes I think I even thrived on the challenge of it. My work was important to me, and I was great at it. But my body was telling a different story. It was finally saying, "enough is enough." I had been diagnosed with a combination of Hashimoto's Hypothyroid Disease and Adrenal Fatigue. I had zapped my body of most of its strength and energy from being in a constant state of stress. When a person's body is under stress, it mimics the 'fight or flight' scenario. After repeatedly doing that over several years, the body simply runs out of steam. Hashimoto's is an autoimmune disease (proven by the presence of a very high number of antibodies in the blood), I received the extra 'bonus' of the disease attacking my own body, which in turn weakened my immune system. My own body was physically attacking itself, and it chose my thyroid as the key target. This had to stop. I had to find some answers and solutions, so I started doing what I do best. I began researching and reading anything and everything I could get my hands on.

I consumed information from websites, medical literature, Dr. Oz, books, and more books. What could I do to get better? What could I take? What should I be eating, or not eating? What activities were recommended? Could my condition even get better? Was there hope? The questions were endless, but I had to know. My doctor gave me several supplements which I took religiously. I had supplements to support my adrenal glands, thyroid, immune system and digestion. She also put me on Natural Dessicated Thyroid (NDT) and took me off of Artificial Synthroid. Suffice it to say that once I switched, the NDT absorbed better which caused me to feel better and have more energy. This was all great, but it was only the beginning.

One of the most important pieces of advice I received over and over from multiple sources was to avoid stress as much as possible. This included both work and personal. So I took that to heart. I started working less hours, taking long walks, connecting with nature, swimming, taking hot relaxing baths, and getting massages. Some nights I would enjoy a glass of wine in the evening, instead of checking my email. I made a list of several activities I enjoyed doing, and would try to do many of those things each week. If someone was upset at work, or stressed out about something, I would remain as calm as I could so that it wouldn't raise my levels. Relaxation was the name of the game and I was going to win at it!

Something else that was emphasized for dealing with an autoimmune disease, was to remove gluten from the diet. My doctor told me that there was a proven connection between the consumption of gluten and the existence of an autoimmune condition. She explained that in order for me to reduce the harmful antibodies, I would need to stop eating gluten. I worked diligently at becoming an expert at reading food labels, figuring out what had gluten in it and what didn't. I became fairly obsessed with my diet and although I fell off the wagon periodically, I did a great job of eliminating gluten from my diet for a long period of time. I was definitely making progress and feeling so much better than I'd felt in a long time. Until I had to work at another four-week trial.

Having horrible numbers on my blood tests and depleted of my energy once again, I knew it was going to take more than what I had done to improve my health for the long-term. That's when I decided that I needed to move. Just move. I needed to move out of Phoenix and head for a smaller town. My intuition told me that I needed to lose the 60-90 minute daily commute to and from my office, and that I needed to be in a place where I was near nature. But, I questioned, "Where?" My long-term boyfriend and I had vacationed in Wyoming, Montana and Colorado the year before. What if I could move to one of those places? I could trade the city for fresh air, mountains, lakes, rivers, and a small town. My intuition was saying, "Yes." And so the elimination process began.

I started applying for jobs. I figured that being a paralegal in a small law firm in a small town would be far less stressful than being a paralegal in a large firm in a large city. I narrowed my sights between the Aspen, Colorado area and Jackson Hole, Wyoming. I had some strong leads in both places and couldn't decide between the two. So, I just let the decision go, and told the Universe to send me where it wanted me to go. As things turned out, the Aspen opportunity fell through. Then the Jackson job fell through. What? I was confused. A couple weeks later, I was looking online and saw a new posting for a position in Jackson. I emailed my resume and within an hour, the lawyer called me. We talked for a bit, and he invited me for an interview. We scheduled it for the following week. Two days later, he called and told me that he was unexpectedly flying to Phoenix. We were talking at a Starbucks near my home just a couple days later. He hired me and told me the job was mine when I moved there. And so the challenge was on.

The next 3 months were a blur. With the help of my daughter and some good friends, I emptied my four bedroom house and put it on the market to lease. It was the perfect opportunity to declutter, sell, and donate lots of stuff that I wouldn't be taking with me. We found a place to live. I gave notice at my job, and said my goodbyes to lots of co-workers and friends. We packed up a U-Haul truck, and my daughter drove out with me. A couple days after, we flew back to Phoenix and I drove my car out, with my two dogs in tow, and the last few things I needed. I called Jackson, Wyoming my new home on May 20, 2013. It was the best decision I could have made for myself. The scenery, nature and wildlife here are exceptional. The air and water are clean and fresh, and the four seasons keep things interesting. I work from home now as a psychic business coach and love it. Traffic is minimal, life is slower paced and stress is low. The perfect combination. My health has never been better, and for that I'm grateful. The road traveled here has been totally worth it. I invite you to listen to your body and decide that you are more than worth it.

KATHY MORTENSON

Kathy Mortenson is an Intuitive Business Coach for women entrepreneurs. She combines business coaching with mindset, divine messages and manifestation to help her clients grow and prosper doing what they love. She's a published co-author in the #1 International Bestseller *My Big Idea Book,* and a children's book author in the making. A lover of the great outdoors, Kathy lives in Jackson Hole, Wyoming and inspires all women to pursue their dreams, create choices in their lives and become the best version of themselves. Expand your business and play a bigger game. Learn more at goddessbusinesscoaching.com.

FAITH, FRIENDS AND FAMILY

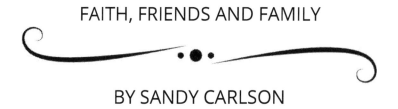

BY SANDY CARLSON

It was July 1995. I was in the shower when I felt the lump. The timing was strange, because my yearly checkup was on the calendar for the following day. That is the day I heard the two words I never wanted to hear again, suspicious and cancer. In reality, my tumor should have been detected on a mammogram the year before; however, machines were not as advanced as they are today and the tumor was deep. Therefore, it was able to grow for over a year to a large 5 cm in size.

Surgery was recommended as soon as possible, so two short weeks later, I found myself having a left radical mastectomy. I was released from the hospital on my 50th birthday. It was a scary time and decisions needed to be made quickly, as the cancer had already spread to seven lymph nodes. Because the cancer was so aggressive, treatment was also aggressive. They shared with me that "big guns" chemo was on the horizon, along with 72 radiation treatments. I survived all of the aggressive treatment and it certainly wasn't easy, but I knew in my heart that God had a greater plan for me. I was placed on an anti-hormone pill daily for nearly eight years. I also started a newer pill with fewer side effects. I have often worried if I should not have changed that drug, because two years later my ribs began to hurt. My Oncologist ordered a bone scan and a biopsy immediately.

It was unbelievable, that after ten years in remission, the same breast cancer had returned to my bones with twelve lesions. I was devastated and couldn't believe it. I embraced my deep faith once again and leaned on what I always refer to as my three "F" words; faith, family and friends! (Matthew 19:26) "With God, all things are possible."

My second recurrence was in 2005 and it is now 2016. My prognosis had originally been to survive for seven years. It has now been 21 years, 4 months and counting. The past 11 years have been a constant attempt with clinical trials, approximately 14 different chemotherapy drugs and more radiation, to keep this cancer stable, as it's still in the bones. We want to keep it away from soft tissue, as the path of a breast cancer recurrence is usually bone, liver, lungs, brain. Once it metastasizes, there's currently no cure, so I'm surviving and enjoying life in all the ways that I can. (Philippians 4:13) "I can do all things through Christ who strengthens me."

My volunteer work has been a way for me to give back, as knowledge becomes power. When you've been diagnosed, it's nice to talk with someone who has walked a similar path before you, to share hope and a warm hug. When I walk into a hospital room, I can tell if the patient is scared, depressed or in denial. Once they meet a survivor though, it makes a lot of difference in the recovery. I always try to leave them with a smile and let them know that they are never alone.

I make myself available to reach out to newly diagnosed breast cancer patients, sharing helpful information as well as a smile, hope and a positive attitude. Life is truly a gift and I thank God for each day, a loving husband and family, and wonderful friends who pray for me daily. I always tell them, "You keep praying, and I'll keep fighting."

I'm very grateful for the life I have and that I can wake up every morning and say, "Yes, I'm still beating it!" In spite of facing these obstacles, I have always made sure I cultivate a positive attitude. My purpose has been to inspire, to provide hope and to serve others on the road to recovery. When you leave others with a smile, they'll know that regardless of their present circumstances, that one day they'll be able to smile too.

SANDY CARLSON

Sandy Carlson is a provider of hope, encouragement and inspiration. She serves with the Reach To Recovery program with the American Cancer Society and has co-chaired a Pink Ribbon Golf Tournament for the past 18 years to help raise funds to advance cancer research. She assists in her family excavating business and is a loving wife, mother and grandmother with a drive to survive.

HEALING THY SELF

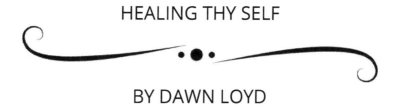

BY DAWN LOYD

All of my life since childhood, I have had huge dreams of what my life was meant to be. What I never realized, was how hard I was trying to protect those dreams, afraid that others could steal them. Even though they couldn't, without my permission, I was holding on tightly to those dreams, as if once I spoke or shared them, the dreams would be gone. What if I was criticized or laughed at? What my dreams were, had nothing to do with making them come true. It was my disbelief that was stopping those very dreams from coming true!

It has taken me fifty-seven years to see this truth. Prior to this awakening, I hadn't understood the power within us and didn't realize how it could impact our health. I can now share with you that I'm living proof that you already have everything inside of you that you need.

I'd like to share a recent experience with you. I walked into the hospital and there were people everywhere. I entered Admissions when a lady, who so rudely stood up and yelled, "I cannot read this hand writing. Will Lacey or whatever the name is please follow me?" I stood up and told her, "I am sorry that you cannot read my name," and I spelled it for her. She then in turn, sends us to another waiting room and said," Wait here and they will call your name."

I glance across the room and a beautiful lady is reading a book. They call out her name and she reaches for her walker, preparing to follow the nurse. I lean over to my daughter and shared, "Look how beautiful that lady is" and she agrees. She really was a beautiful lady and she deserved a miracle. She definitely deserved a better quality of life. While it has always been easy for me to believe that others deserved such miracles, I lacked the same belief for myself. I try to convince myself that I have had many miracles in my life. The truth is, I've experienced more miracles than I can count! As I'm walking down the hallway of the hospital, a divine voice said, "You have just received a miracle." The message is repeated several times as I walk down the hallway.

I had come down with the flu for the first time in 27 years. I went to the doctor unwillingly, but I had no choice because I wasn't getting any better. They prescribed antibiotics and I began feeling a bit better. A couple of months later, I started hearing something different in my breathing; however, no one else could hear it, so I thought maybe it was just my imagination since I am the only one that can hear it. As I was sitting quietly, the divine voice tells me over and over, to go to the doctor. My mind wanders back to the previous two months. My energy levels had dropped drastically, but I discount it because I hadn't been eating right and exercising as I know I am supposed to. I continue dismissing the voice inside of me. I learned to tune into my divine voice when I became a life coach a few years ago. The voice just kept saying, "Go to the doctor," so after a few days of listening to the voice, I decided to make an appointment. As it turns out, it was perfect timing as my life was saved.

At my appointment, the doctor looks at me with bewilderment as I explain that I was only there as a precaution. She then laughs and says, "It's ok, as it is better to be safe than sorry." She hears absolutely nothing. I keep insisting, because the voice is persistent that they keep looking. I then began having heart palpations, so they ran an EKG and a breathing test. The tests turn out great and they send me home. I still wasn't content so they finally agreed to do an x-ray on my lungs. The nurse asks lots of questions such as, "Are you coughing or having any problems breathing?" I had no problems breathing up until now.

I go back to the examining room to see the doctor again. The doctor seems baffled as four doctors have conducted exams and heard nothing wrong with my breathing. This doctor walked in and said, "Well, there is something abnormal on your right lower lung," but she did not know what was wrong. All she knew was that the x-ray was displaying something white that was pushing on my right lower lung. Up until now, my blood pressure had been great but all of a sudden my blood pressure is sky high. The doctor sends me to get a cat scan a few days later. I make an appointment once again to get the results and check my blood pressure. I am diagnosed with a hernia on top of my stomach and intestines and the doctor mentions she's never seen anything like it. An older doctor says he has only seen it twice. Apparently this is more common with babies, but not adults.

They contact a surgeon and he refuses to touch it, but recommends a surgeon in a nearby state. They schedule me an appointment for three weeks later. As I waited for the surgery, my quality of life begins declining rapidly. In desperation, I see the first surgeon who said the only way he would do it is if another surgeon, who is a heart and lung specialist, would do it with him. He explains that my intestines and stomach are in my chest, above my breast! He then goes on to tell me that he wants me to meet the other surgeon. Before I leave, he says, "If you have any pain at all, get to a hospital that has a helicopter, because where you live, the hospitals are not set up for the trauma that is going on within you." He mentioned he wanted the second surgeon there because he couldn't risk problems with my lungs or heart during the surgery. I'm told that they'll need to cut me under my breasts and on my side. They attempt to hold off on performing the surgery for over a month later.

Then, one night my daughter woke me up saying that I was gasping for air trying to breathe. I was experiencing heart palpations, extreme headaches from lack of oxygen and couldn't seem to function at all. The doctors attempt to keep putting the surgery off, but the divine voice kept telling me to push forward in getting the surgery as soon as possible. Finally, the surgery was moved up, the first surgeon backed out, but the second surgeon followed through.

I am truly blessed to this day to be alive. We all have everything we need within us that will guide us through our entire lives. Every step of the way, the divine within me actually saved my life and it never wavered in guiding me. After the surgery, the surgeon shared with me that I was born with this. My intestines and stomach were in a sack, pressing against my heart and lungs, taking a major toll on my body. It's surprising I was successfully able to birth three children, so I know they are also my miracles.

I now believe all of this happened for a reason and have discovered a new passion, purpose and meaning for my life, as I reach out to help others. Each of us has a story, and the story needs to be told. Telling your story allows others to heal, so I can guarantee that someone, somewhere needs to hear it.

Listen to the divine voice within, as it knows you. I could have listened to the rude lady, I could have listened to the numerous doctors that couldn't hear anything, or the various tests that couldn't locate what was wrong, but I knew the divine voice doesn't steer us wrong. If we are still here, then we still have more work to do, more people to serve. You have a purpose to fulfill, so please dare to **dream boldly**.

DAWN LOYD

Dawn Loyd is a speaker, author, life coach and creator of Destined 2 Dawn. She uses Psych-K to facilitate change that creates a powerful impact. Destined 2 Dawn assists in shifting your perception to successfully reach your target and helps clients in finding the missing peace in their limiting beliefs. You are not your story, nor your past. You are truly destined to live the life of your dreams. All of your answers are within. Elevate, expand and evolve into all that you were meant to be. Connect with Dawn at Destined2Dawn@hotmail.com.

GOING DEEP, TO GO WIDE

BY VIVIANA MEDEL

"This is it," I often thought during my many months laid up in bed, barely able to walk. Each day, I felt my life force dwindling and hope right along with it. I wasn't very religious but I did sleep with the Bible, thinking it would shield me from whatever dark force had taken hold of me. I wasn't ready to leave this life yet.

The fear coursing through my veins was excruciating. At the time, I didn't know I was experiencing a severe case of adrenal fatigue, but I was painfully aware of what led up to it. A series of unfortunate events, as Lemony Snicket might say. Or were they?

At the core, I wasn't living an authentic life. I desired a life that reflected the light inside of me, rather than one crafted out of the expectations of others, society, my culture, my gender, my age, my weight, my color, my religion (or lack thereof), my pets, my car, my alma mater, my music, my you fill in the blank. Label after label, box after box, all drowning under the heaviness of conditioned and limiting beliefs devoid of purpose, passion, and joy.

I was not an unaware person before this happened. In fact, I spoke often about being an extension of the divine, a bigger picture at play, the ONEness of it all. All lip service, for I kept muddling through still believing in all the emotional, psychological, and physical abuse I had experienced up to that moment. Constantly criticized? Check. Punished? Check. Abandoned? Check. Unsupported? Check. Failed relationships, jobs, dreams? Check, check, check.

The "voice" inside my head, the conglomeration of all my conditioning, was so very present. I could feel its pull on me daily. The stress building in my body as the chasm between expectation, laden with perfectionism, and what my conscious self knew to be true grew wider and wider. It is not as if I wasn't constantly receiving the message to step back and allow life to flow through me, but I did not listen. The fear of not living up to all the "shoulds," "musts," and "have tos," in life kept me on a downward spiral, but the universe had other plans and did what it needed to do.

It struck me in the head with a cosmic 2 x 4 and did it ever hurt! I was left reeling for months on end. You've never seen someone attempting to backpedal so fast in your life, but it was futile. As any good conditioned girl would do, I spent copious amounts of time coddling the victim persona. "Why me?" and

"How did this happen?" kept having a sing-song each day. Resentment, anger, frustration, sadness, grief had become my besties. Crying (make that wailing) was a daily guarantee, and all of this internal turmoil digging its way out of the recesses of my psyche took me down, and fast! My body started to slow down, my adrenal glands were depleted and starving for a much needed respite. The choice was made for me. I had to get quiet.

My body became the physical manifestation of how I had lived my life. Not expressing my full self. Not speaking my truth. Being a people pleaser, a doormat, and a pushover; agreeing to things I did not want to do out of expectation, loneliness, and fear. I was an emotional wreck on the inside. I was crying over why I couldn't have the life I desired. Why did others make it and I did not? Why did _____ (fill in the blank with your favorite victim mentality excuse).

Emotions are a surge of energy. Emotions at their core are Energy in *motion*. They need to move, to breathe, and to be expressed. Suppressing them when they surged, to then attempt to release them later, only stressed my body. It could no longer support this pattern of behavior. My adrenals burnt out and I no longer had the luxury of being a closet drama queen.

Once I was laid up in bed, I literally could not express my

emotions in a physical way. I still felt the terror. I still had my tortured mind asking umpteen questions. I still felt the need to cry and grieve, to feel angry and frustrated, but I couldn't express any of it. Any surge of emotional energy weakened my body further. At first, this caused me great despair, for I felt trapped in all the turbulence, but it soon became clear that stillness was my way out.

Answers will not come to a chaotic mind, so over the next few months, I focused what little energy I had, to go within. In the silence, I could feel my inner compass and be shown what I needed to know. I started to expand once again and allow another perspective, the truth, to flow into my life. This was the door that led to my reawakening.

Quieting my mind increased the feeling of peace and when at peace, the body could heal. I supported its healing journey with herbals, homeopathy, flower essences, energy work, meditation, yoga, and connecting to like-minded individuals who expanded my awareness of self even more.

Stopping judgment and letting go were paramount to my recovery. I realized that the conditioned mind only had my past experiences to go on. It desired nothing more than to keep me safe, by thriving on fear and doing everything in its power to keep me where I was; stuck, feeling alone, separate, and unworthy. Once I stepped back from that mindset and went within, the quieter I became, the more expansion I allowed. It was clear to me that all I had ever judged as being against me; the "unfortunate events," were not unfortunate at all. Everything I had experienced (and was to experience in my lifetime) came with a blessing. I received the gift of clarity.

Clarity of purpose, of beingness, of realizing that whatever did not keep me in a state of peace, was a lie. A fabrication of my conditioned mind to keep me safe, fearful, and playing small. This knowing was the portal to stepping into a greater version of my one true self, time and time again.

The stronger my body got, the more I could release all the emotional duress that had led me to my dark night of the soul. I threw it all into the fire of self-discovery, for it would only burn what I was not. This was the beginning of remembering the divine within and that everything and everyone was a part of me. I was part of the OneSelf.

Since that time, my awareness has expanded exponentially. I am more embodied, grounded, following my dreams and desires, but most of all **I am free**. Free to live an authentic life following my inner guidance, being present and fulfilling my soul's purpose. Free to live from my heart and not my head. Free to be the wondrous expression of the divine I am. Free to simply be. The light within me, is also within you. Dare to let go of it all. A life of freedom awaits you.

"You are not a drop in the ocean; you are the entire ocean in one drop." - Rumi

VIVIANA MEDEL

Viviana Medel is a flower essence and energy alchemist for women who desire more balance and freedom in their lives. Through her intuitive readings, inspirational blog posts, flower essence blends, and energy work, she's here to remind you of the wholeness of your being, while making it all feel like faerie magic! Her thoughts on life and the universe have been featured in Wild Sister magazine, guest podcasts and blogs. Her loving clients have called her "an amazing healer" and "angel" and have deemed her as "very wise." She enjoys creative cooking, reading mind-bending novels, yoga and her cats. Get ready to experience magic at FloweringGoddess.com.

A MIRACULOUS HEALING

BY ANNE ARNDT

I still remember my eleven-year-old fidgety body, trying so hard to sit still in that hard wooden pew at Sunday mass. Wondering when the service would be over, I turned my eyes toward the priest and decided to try to decipher his words in order to help the time pass. What I heard next didn't seem to need deciphering though.

I almost couldn't believe my ears as the priest read these words from the gospel of John, "Very truly I tell you, whoever believes in me will do the works I have been doing, and they will do even greater things than these, because I am going to the Father." (John 14:12)

Both the priest and God had my full attention now. We can help others heal, just the way Jesus did? I was excited, really excited! Even as a little girl, I knew I wanted to help others to heal and be happy in this life. I was blown away that Jesus himself would tell us that we could share in the healing works he had done, and more. More? My mind couldn't fathom what more there might be.

The next words I heard out of the priest's mouth excited me even more, "For where two or three gather in my name, there am I with them" (Matthew 18:20) he said. I didn't think the news from the gospel of John could be topped. But it was. You mean we can do what Jesus did and he will be there *with us* too? God got a whole lot more real that Sunday for me at church.

I didn't know what to do with this news at the time, but I sure was excited that Jesus was available when we gathered in his name and that people could do the things he had done while he was on the Earth. It would be more than 13 years before I would say those words from the gospel of John and Matthew out loud.

One day while working at a spiritual gift, book, and music store, a woman named Michelle came in and I asked if I could help her. She was looking for some soothing and relaxing music because she was having surgery the next day.

Mary, the owner of the store, came up from the back of the store to help us as we looked through the selection of music. Mary, being the very social woman she was, asked what we were looking for and why. Michelle and Mary began talking and as Mary always did so well, she got Michelle to open up further about the nature of the surgery.

Michelle shared that she was having surgery to remove a significant lump in her breast that the doctors thought was cancerous. Michelle told us that she had been doing some intense inner work, prayer, and soul searching ever since she discovered the lump. I left the conversation a couple of minutes in to help another customer.

A few minutes later, Mary called, "Annie, we need you. We are going to pray with Michelle." After finishing with the customer I was helping, I felt myself hesitantly walk over to the middle of the store where Mary, Michelle, and two other women, also employees of the store, were waiting. We all held hands and began to pray.

I found myself nervous and hesitant about praying with everyone. I asked myself why I was feeling this way, especially because the prayer was in service of Michelle and her surgery tomorrow. What was going on inside of me I wondered? The answer came and it was the remnants of a Catholic upbringing that had left me with feelings of guilt and shame, like something was always the "matter with me."

I wasn't sure if I could, "do it right" when praying out loud for Michelle with everyone watching and listening. I didn't know what God wanted for her life. How could I ask God to heal her if that wasn't what he wanted? I was focusing on myself and my fears, instead of opening up in service of this dear woman we were praying for.

When it came time for me to pray, I knew I had to step out of myself and just open up to God. I knew I wanted to just be present with Michelle and with God. So, I prayed, "God, I just open to you and pray for Michelle's healing, however that looks to you, God. Jesus told us that when two or more are gathered in His name, that He is there with us. He also said when He healed people, that we too could do what He did, and more. I just pray for Michelle's healing, whatever that means God. Thank you for bringing Michelle here."

As I finished those last words, something began to transform within my body. I received a mental picture of the inside of my body and it was lit up. It looked like an empty mine shaft with light shooting down from the top to illuminate it. I had never seen or imagined anything like it.

The best way I can describe what I felt in my left breast a second later, is to say that an intense and powerful shock of electricity surged through it. It looked and felt like a mini bolt of lightning. I was surprised, overwhelmed, and confused. I didn't understand what had just happened.

I was the last to pray, so we broke the circle a couple of

seconds later and I ran behind the cash register and started sobbing uncontrollably. The tears didn't stop for several minutes. I remember so clearly that I wasn't scared; just confused and overwhelmed.

A few minutes later, as Mary helped me to gain control of myself, Michelle came over to say goodbye. When Michelle said her goodbye, I heard very clearly in my mind, "Make sure they check before the surgery, make sure they check before the surgery. Make sure they check."

What did this mean, I thought? Then I got it. The message was to let Michelle know to ask the doctors to check that the lump was still there before they did the surgery. Before I shared the message with her, my curiosity just had to ask, "Which breast was the lump in?" Michelle said, "the left." Relieved in my mind as some sense was being made of what had just happened, I shared the message with her about asking the doctors to make sure the lump was still there before doing the surgery. She assured me she would ask them to check.

Two days later, Michelle called the store and I answered the phone. She let me know that when the doctor checked her breast before the surgery, the lump was gone. The doctors performed a couple more tests and then declared that whatever was there before, was now gone. Michelle thanked me and all of the women who prayed with her.

To this day, I am not sure whether the experience with Michelle was simply an affirmation that she was already healed through the work and prayer she had done on her own or if the healing happened right then and there in the store, as we all prayed for her. All I know is that God does the healing and all we need to do is the asking.

Since that day with Michelle, I have participated in and witnessed many more miraculous healings. Sometimes we forget to call on God until we need help picking up the shattered pieces of our lives. It can be difficult to remember that God is here to guide and help us through each day of our lives if we allow Him. God is right here, right now.

So that I may never forget that He is here for me and with me, I say this prayer each day:

Dear God, Thank you for this precious life. Today, I ask you Father to give me the thoughts to think, the words to say, and the actions to take, in order to serve you and this world in the highest way possible. I love you. Amen.

ANNE ARNDT

Anne Arndt, M.A. is a transformational coach, mentor, intuitive and registered psychotherapist. She's answering the call to guide and support people in awakening to the truth of who they are and what they came here to do. Anne has been guiding people back home to themselves for over 17 years. She works one-on-one with clients over the phone and in person. She also facilitates healing and transformational workshops. Anne offers a safe space for people to explore, grow, and ultimately transform, so that they are free to live life as their truest, most authentic self. Her greatest joy is watching people step beyond fear and limitation into authentic expression and limitless possibility! Learn more at www.sensitivementor.com.

THANK YOU!

We sincerely hope you've enjoyed the sharing of our hearts, the messages of hope, and our deepest desires, as we've accepted the dare to dream boldly. We hope you'll join us! These final pages are dedicated to help guide you, as you boldly declare your 100 dreams in 10 days (of your choosing), to expand and awaken the power that is about to be unlocked from deep within you. The prompts are available as a key to ignite your deepest desires. They aren't meant to keep you in a "box" though, so feel free to get creative and dream until your heart is content.

Download free templates to declare your dreams at www.CarrieStepp.com/dream-boldly.

MY 100 BOLD DREAMS

INSPIRATION: I AM ACHIEVING _____ THIS YEAR.

1.

2.

3.

4.

5.

6.

7.

8.

9.

10.

INSPIRATION: I AM SERVING + GIVING...

11.

12.

13.

14.

15.

16.

17.

18.

19.

20.

INSPIRATION: I AM FORGIVING...

21.

22.

23.

24.

25.

26.

27.

28.

29.

30.

INSPIRATION: MY HEALTH + WELLNESS GOALS

31.

32.

33.

34.

35.

36.

37.

38.

39.

40.

INSPIRATION: MY LOVE + RELATIONSHIPS DREAMS

41.

42.

43.

44.

45.

46.

47.

48.

49.

50.

INSPIRATION: MY CAREER + LIFE PURPOSE DREAMS

51.

52.

53.

54.

55.

56.

57.

58.

59.

60.

INSPIRATION: MY FINANCIAL ABUNDANCE

61.

62.

63.

64.

65.

66.

67.

68.

69.

70.

INSPIRATION: LOCATIONS I AM PLANNING TO VISIT

71.

72.

73.

74.

75.

76.

77.

78.

79.

80.

INSPIRATION: DREAMS FOR MY CHILDREN/GRANDCHILDREN

81.

82.

83.

84.

85.

86.

87.

88.

89.

90.

INSPIRATION: ALL OF MY DREAMS ARE COMING TRUE!

91.

92.

93.

94.

95.

96.

97.

98.

99.

100.